# 100 Great Thai Dishes

# 100 Great Thai Dishes

Photography by Neil Barclay

First published in Great Britain in 2005 by Cassell Illustrated,
A division of Octopus Publishing Group Limited,
2–4 Heron Quays, London E14 4JP

This edition published in 2008

A CIP catalogue record for this book is available from the
British Library.

ISBN 1 84403 636 3
EAN 978 1 84403 636 3

Edited by Victoria Alers-Hankey and Robin Douglas-Withers
Photography by Neil Barclay
Prop Styling by Fanny Ward
Design by DW Design
Art Direction by Jo Knowles

Printed in China

# Acknowledgments

I would like to thank my grandmother for giving me all the best things in life, and who was largely responsible for my interest, knowledge, and know-how in preserving and creating Thai recipes. Thanks also go to my mother for her endless encouragement and support. Her belief in me has always been phenomenal. She has taught me to be positive and stand up for what I believe in. And, as for my father, his financial support throughout my schooling years abroad gave me the opportunity to be in many different parts of the world and to understand and accept each culture as it comes. Last but not least, my very special thanks to my young son, Timothy, for his wonderful praises and frank criticisms of my cooking! He is my greatest inspiration in all I do.

Thai food has played a huge role in my life. It is one of the few subjects that I can talk passionately about – it's in my blood and soul. I hope you will be able to feel even half the enjoyment that I get from it. For me, 'Life is a real blessing when work becomes a pleasure.'

# Contents

# Introduction

Thai food is well known for its evocative aromas, subtle blends of herbs and spices, and its contrasting tastes and textures. It is a wonderfully unusual and sophisticated style of cooking that has been influenced heavily by other countries, such as Peru and Mexico in South America, China, India, and Portugal. Chiles, for example, were introduced from South America, as originally we used peppercorns to make food spicy. The taste of Thai food is a testament to all these influences: It can be plain or fancy, and varies from region to region, yet retains a distinctive identity.

Some of the recipes in this book were created by me especially for the menu at my restaurant, the Busabong in London. They were inspired by other cuisines, but altered to include Thai herbs and ingredients. Others were adapted from original Thai recipes to reflect my personal tastes and preferences, such as Thai Duckling (page 85), Crispy Soft-shell Crab with Chile and Holy Basil (page 86) and Spicy Tuna Salad with Lemongrass (page 49). These can be identified throughout the book by my signature next to the recipe heading. I am proud to say that many of these dishes have become best-sellers on the Busabong menu!

In Thailand we put several dishes on the table to be eaten together, so it is important to choose dishes that will make a delicious and well-balanced meal. A Thai meal has to be a sensuous experience: It involves so many pleasurable senses—sight, smell, taste—and an irresistible blend of flavors which should leave you longing for more. Most spicy, strongly flavored main dishes need rice to accompany them as this tempers their flavor. Snacks and Thai salads are usually served alongside the main dishes, but are not eaten with rice. This traditional way of presenting a Thai meal helps you control the amount you eat, as everything is there in front of you. In a Thai meal there are usually two courses, a savory one and a sweet one. Snacks and desserts are also often eaten between meals. It is normal for a Thai to munch all day long, but dinner is our one proper meal of the day. It is an opportunity for all the family to meet and chat about their day. Mealtimes give us a sense of togetherness and unity, a time to enjoy each other's company. In Thailand, when our friends visit, or when we meet, we usually ask if they have eaten yet, rather than asking them how they are. This may sound amazing, but it's just the way the Thais are!

The secret of Thai cooking is to know how to combine spices, herbs, and seasonings to create a harmonious taste—this is simply down to your knowledge and experience in the use of Thai ingredients. To this end, I have also included a few tips on what to do and what not to do when making Thai food, and on the ingredients used, to help you remember which herbs and spices go in which dish. That's it, Thai food made simple to suit your busy lifestyle. I hope the recipes in this book will be a real breath of fresh air to anyone who wants to make authentic Thai food with little time and minimum effort without compromising the flavor, originality, or authenticity.

 Mini C

# Tools, Techniques, and Tips

## Tools

In a modern Thai kitchen, simple tools and equipment are used. When a tool is misplaced, we often make one up from what we find around the house. At one time I did not have a steamer, so used a deep pot of water and a stainless-steel strainer instead. It worked perfectly! There are a few things, however, that will make your life much easier if you have them.

- Blender and/or food processor
- Chopping block
- Sharp cleaver
- Electric rice cooker
- Sharp vegetable knife
- Pestle and mortar
- Strainer
- Steamer
- Wok and spatula

## Techniques

### Preparation

For stir-fries and curry dishes, beef and pork are always thinly sliced across the grain to make the meat less chewy, unless you are using salted beef or shredded beef, which should be sliced lengthwise in the same direction as the grain. For stewing, meat should be cut into chunky pieces.

For most chicken and duck recipes, the flesh is already tender, and so they should always be thinly sliced lengthwise in the same direction as the grain.

Thais tend to eat their beef and shrimp while they are still quite rare. In fact, sometimes they eat shrimp that are still alive. Chicken, duck, and pork, however, are always well cooked. Lamb is hardly ever used in Thai cooking because it has a strong smell that competes with other flavors.

Before cooking shrimp, twist off their heads, then pull off the shells, leaving the tails on. To devein a shrimp, use a small knife to slit the back from head to tail, then lift out the thin dark cord. Leaving the tail on your shrimp will make it easier to tell when they are cooked as the tail is brighter pink than the rest of the body. It also helps anyone who is not that keen on shrimp to spot them, and avoid putting them on their plate!

To make your ready-made curry paste more aromatic, stir-fry it with vegetable oil and a few kaffir lime leaves. Most chefs add in extra freshly ground herbs and spices, such as chiles, galangal, lemongrass, and shallots to make it unique.

If you are using dried noodles in a noodle dish, it is best to soak them first in cold water for 2 hours. Soaking them in warm or hot water might be quicker, but will cause the noodles to break into small pieces when they are stir-fried.

All Thai salads must be assembled immediately before serving, never in advance. The chopping and cutting of ingredients can be done ahead of time, but the actual mixing must be left until the last minute. If you are making a warm salad, seasonings such as fish sauce, sugar, and lemon juice can be stirred straight into the salad as the heat of the dish will melt the sugar. However, if the salad does not include a cooked ingredient, mix the seasoning well before it is added to the salad to make sure that the sugar is completely dissolved.

### Cooking

When I say "stir-fry," I mean you should carefully use a spatula to lift and turn over the food. This stops the delicate ingredients such as noodles or fish from being broken up.

When using a wok, the heat is concentrated in the center of the pan, which is also where all the food is. This is why you must keep turning the food to prevent it from burning. Instead of constantly adjusting the heat level, you can also lift the wok up away from the heat as you stir.

When stir-frying rice noodles in a dish that does not use an egg, the wok must be pre-heated until very hot to stop the noodles from sticking. Turn the heat to medium, then add the oil and the noodles. If eggs are being used in a noodle dish, heat the oil in the wok, then add the meat. The eggs should go in as soon as the meat is cooked, but before the noodles are added. This way the eggs will be well cooked and a little brown. If the noodles are fresh, don't put too much oil in at the start, but add it little by little if they stick to the wok.

When stir-frying vegetables, use a medium-high heat to maintain their crispness. Add the slowest-cooking vegetables first, followed by the quick-cooking ones.

If you've pre-stir-fried your curry paste with oil, and use coconut cream to stir-fry your meat with, you won't need to add any extra oil.

For a Thai curry, the meat is first fried with curry paste (pre-fried with oil) and coconut cream, to tenderize it. Thinner coconut milk is then added to make the curry sauce.

If a curry becomes too dry while simmering, add water, not coconut milk, as coconut milk will make the curry too thick.

When your curry has achieved the right texture, a layer of oil will emerge on the surface. This comes from the oil used to pre-fry your curry paste and the coconut cream. It is not always a sign that the curry is ready, as if you are making a fish or vegetable curry, these ingredients should be added last, after the oil has risen, to make sure they are not overcooked.

Take special care not to overcook seafood in curry dishes—always add fish or shellfish at the last stage of cooking any curry so that they do not become chewy and overcooked.

When deep frying frozen pre-made snacks, such as spring rolls, they will float to the top of the oil when they are ready.

## Tips

### Serving sizes

Because Thai food is hardly ever served in individual portions and is usually shared, it is difficult to be exact on serving sizes. For this reason it is easier to say that each recipe will serve approximately four people as part of a meal with three other main dishes, plus enough rice for four.

### Seasonings and flavors

All my recipes are based on my personal preferences, and reflect how they are cooked in my restaurant, the Busabong. However, there are a few things that you should bear in mind:

Always use homemade stock, made with white cabbage (for vegetarians) or chicken bones. Do not add seasoning. If you do not have any cabbage or chicken, use plain water when a recipe calls for stock. Highly aromatic vegetables, such as celery and onion, are not suitable to make stock for Thai recipes, as they will overpower the other flavors.

Thai fish sauce is not the same as fish stock.

You should never sprinkle cilantro leaves on any Thai curries, the exception being Massaman Curry with Lamb (page 61).

Never substitute galangal with ginger.

# Ingredients

Thai food would not be Thai food without all the aromatic herbs and spices. The most common ones are listed here, along with a description of their properties and uses. If you are going to become a keen Thai chef, you should keep all these in your refrigerator.

Nowadays it is becoming much simpler to find all Thai ingredients as more Asian supermarkets are opening up and even local supermarkets have quite a good stock. It's a good idea to make your shopping list before you visit a Thai supermarket, as not only might the storekeepers not have time to help you, but they might not know the English name for what you are looking for. I have included the Thai pronunciation for the most commonly used ingredients to help you.

Preparing a well-balanced Thai meal for four people should not take hours if you are smart enough to take advantage of ready-made ingredients such as curry paste or fish paste. Most Thai restaurants use ready-made curry paste, and simply enhance it with their preferred choice of herbs.

Understanding how and when to add your herbs and spices, or any simple ingredients, is just as vital as the cooking itself. For example, lemon and lime juice are never added to a dish while it is cooking, as the aroma evaporates, leaving a bitter taste. Instead the juice is usually the last thing to be added to a dish. Aromatic pastes, such as curry pastes or garlic and chile paste, should always be stir-fried with oil first, taking care not to burn them, so that their full aroma is released before the other ingredients are added.

## Herbs, Spices, and Other Thai Flavorings

### Banana leaf (*Bai-Tong*)

This is a very useful leaf that has a smoky and light fragrance. Traditionally, banana leaves were used for wrapping food and they are still useful for holding food for steamed dishes, or to wrap around food that will be baked or broiled. The leaves give off a smoky smell when heated under a broiler.

### Holy basil (*Bai Gra-Prao*)

This is a very pungent, aromatic plant commonly used in stir-fries with fresh chiles and garlic. The leaves are light-green in color and slightly hairy, and only release their aroma on frying. A few non-coconut milk-based curries also include fresh holy basil, such as Aromatic Chicken Jungle Curry (page 60). The coconut milk-based curries usually use sweet basil or no basil at all. Holy basil reduces digestive gases and can ease coughing.

### Sweet basil (*Bai Ho-Ra-Pa*)

This is similar to Italian basil, and is used in many curry dishes. The stems are usually a red-purple color. The leaves are aromatic, but not overpowering in flavor, so they complement most curries. The leaves are often eaten raw with appetizers such as spring rolls and can also be added to spicy salads. You can use normal Italian basil as a substitute. Sweet basil soothes and settles the stomach and can help with indigestion, gastritis, and cramps. Other beneficial properties include clearing the skin and easing respiratory problems. Sweet basil leaves are also believed to help prevent cancer and heart conditions.

### Chiles (Prik)

The Portuguese introduced chiles to Thailand in the sixteenth century. Before then, fresh peppercorns were used to add spiciness to food. *Prik-Khee-noo*, also known as bird's eye chiles, are the hottest. As a general rule, the smaller the chiles, the hotter they are—as we say in Thai, *Lek Prik-Khee-Noo*, which means "small, but dangerous." Seeding chiles can reduce their spiciness without taking away their aromatic aroma or flavor. If you can't find fresh chiles, use dried chile powder, but not chile sauce. Chile powder does not have any extra ingredients mixed into it that interfere with the taste of what you are cooking—the aroma of the dish might be slightly different, but it will still be acceptable. Chiles contain capsaicin, an active ingredient beneficial to the respiratory system. When eaten in moderation, they are known to stimulate blood circulation and be beneficial in preventing heart disease and cancer. Eating too much spicy food, however, is believed to inhibit the absorption of nutrients.

### Dried chiles (Prik Hang)

Chile powder is made from roasted dried chiles. When dried chiles are roasted, the smell is irresistible. Dried chiles are often sprinkled over spicy salads and noodle soups. The degree of spiciness really depends on the types of chiles you use—the smaller, the spicier. Their nutritional properties are the same as those of fresh chiles.

### Cilantro leaves (Bai Pauk-Chee), stalks/roots (Raak Pauk-Chee)

Every part of the cilantro plant is used in Thai cooking. The leaves are generally used for garnishing. The roots include all of the green stems, and are pounded together with garlic to make a paste. The aroma of cilantro roots is extremely strong and Thailand is one of very few countries that use this particular part of the plant in cooking. It aids digestion.

### Coconut milk (Naam-Ga-Ti), coconut cream (Hua-Ga-Ti)

Coconut milk is one of the main ingredients in Thai curries and it adds sweetness to dishes. It comes from ripe brown coconuts, rather than young green ones, that have very little water left in them. The green ones are for drinking from and their flesh is used to make desserts, or combined with their

juice as a drink. Coconut cream is made from the first squeeze of grated ripe coconut flesh mixed with warm water. Coconut milk comes when the cream is mixed with the thin, watery liquid from the rest of the squeezes. With canned coconut milk, the creamy part normally sits at the top with the watery part underneath. Don't shake the can if you need to keep them separate—a Thai curry should not be too thick as it is eaten with rice, which is meant to absorb the sauce. Nowadays coconut milk is widely available in most supermarkets. For watery types of Thai dessert you can use a carton of coconut milk, but for desserts where you need just the cream you will need to use canned coconut milk so that you can separate off the cream. Coconut milk is a source of natural energy, but it does contain high levels of saturated fat, which is easy to burn off through exercise.

Cilantro roots (*Raak Pauk-Chee*)

### Coriander seeds (Med Pauk-Chee)

These are normally mixed with cumin seeds. The seeds are roasted and pounded together to make a powder and used in some marinades such as satay (page 29), or to make more Indian-, Malaysian- or Indonesian-influenced curry pastes. The seeds aid digestion, preventing the build-up of digestive gases.

### Curry paste (Naam-Prik-Gang)

There are many varieties of curry paste—green, red, orange, and yellow—and all are used for making different curries. Some contain more herbs, while others have more spices. It depends where in Thailand a particular curry originates as to which paste is used. Ready-made curry pastes are available in most Asian foodstores and supermarkets. To enhance the aroma of your paste, stir-fry the curry paste in vegetable oil, adding extra herbs or spices to taste. Once the paste has cooled down, it can be stored in an airtight container in the refrigerator for up to about 3 months.

### Fermented/salted soybeans (Tao-Jiew)

These add great flavor to noodle dishes such as Fried Rice Vermicelli with Coconut Milk (page 124). They are also used in a few steamed dishes with ginger. As they are quite salty, you must be careful when using them with fish sauces. You can buy them in jars at most Asian supermarkets; if you can't find them, there aren't really any substitutes, so just leave them out.

### Fish sauce (Naam-Pla)

This everyday condiment is made from saltwater fish, water, and salt and provides the salty taste in Thai food. If you are a vegetarian, salt is an acceptable substitute, but does not have the same punch. When you buy Thai fish sauce, choose one that is a clear, light brown in color. If you see deposits at the bottom of the bottle, it has been sitting on the shelf for too long. Bottles with plastic caps are also more hygienic. Light soy sauce is another acceptable replacement, but it does give a different aroma. Fish sauce is high in protein, vitamins, and minerals.

### Galangal (Kha)

This root is very distinctive in aroma and taste. It is often mistaken for ginger because they look similar, but ginger is not a substitute for galangal. Galangal is used in both of the Lemongrass Soups on pages 35 and 37. If you cannot find it, increase the other ingredients to make the dish more aromatic. Galangal helps ease indigestion and rheumatism, and contains oils such as eugenal, cineol, and camphor. These help stimulate digestion and reduce flatulence. It is also used to soothe infected tonsils and to clear the throat of phlegm.

Galangal (Kha)

### Garlic (Gra-Tiam)

Thai garlic is very strong in taste and aroma. It comes in much smaller cloves than western garlic and is used in most Thai dishes. However, the quantities given in all the recipes are for western garlic. In Thai cooking, the cloves are usually pounded rather than cut as pounding is the best method for releasing the aroma. The only substitute for fresh garlic is chopped garlic in oil or garlic paste in a tube. Garlic is well known for its many medicinal properties, such as aiding digestion, preventing gas, easing respiratory problems, and lowering cholesterol levels.

### Ginger (Khing)

This is used for both savory and sweet dishes and hot and cold drinks. Grated ginger is used in some stir-fried dishes and thinly sliced ginger is used as an accompaniment to appetizers. Be careful if you use both ginger and chiles in the same dish as they bring different types of spiciness and hotness. Ginger is high in iron and vitamin C, and it has been used for centuries as a medicine to lower cholesterol, cleanse the body, alleviate sore throats, relieve colic and diarrhea, and help digestion.

### Aromatic ginger *(Kra-Chai)*

This is often used in fish and shellfish dishes with a curry paste base in order to reduce the fishy smell. Green curries with fish, fish balls, or shrimp tend to include fresh aromatic ginger, and it is one of the main ingredients in Aromatic Chicken Jungle Curry (page 60), and also makes a great drink (page 134). It can relieve stomach pains, contains anti-flatulence agents, eases coughing, and has antimicrobial properties.

Aromatic ginger *(Kra-Chai)*

Kaffir lime *(Louk Ma-Grood)*

15

It can also help to overpower any fishy smell in a dish, and is used in aromatic, spicy Thai salads. There is no substitute for lemongrass. The inner layers give more aroma than the outer layers. Lightly pounding the stalks and boiling them in water makes a wonderful, refreshing drink, hot or cold (page 133). The oil of lemongrass is often used in aromatherapy and is a good cure for an upset stomach and indigestion.

### Kaffir lime *(Louk Ma-Grood)*, kaffir lime leaf *(Bai Ma-Grood)*

Thais tend to use the leaves more than the fruit for cooking, as they are highly aromatic. They can't, however, be replaced with lime juice, so just omit them if you can't find them. Kaffir lime rind is often included in curry pastes and the juice is used in some curry dishes to add a gentle, sour taste. If you squeeze the fruit in your hand, the rind releases oil, which is used to make a shampoo that helps cure dandruff and makes hair shine. Kaffir limes keep the skin healthy and are known to help relieve stomach pain.

### Lemongrass *(Ta-Krai)*

Lemongrass has a very distinctive, lemony taste and aroma that gives a fresh taste to some of the more spicy soups.

Lemongrass *(Ta-Krai)*

### Lime (Ma-Noaw)

Lime juice is used in most Thai salads. It has a sharper taste than lemon juice. A dash of lime juice with fish sauce and chiles makes a popular Thai sauce called *naam-pla-prik* (Spicy Fish Sauce, page 76), often used on rice. Lime juice helps reduce inflammation, aids digestion, and eases coughing. Most of my recipes use lemon juice, however, as it's easier to find outside Thailand.

### Mint (Sa-Ra-Nae)

Mint is usually used in spicy Thai salads and is served alongside some of the appetizers. Its oil has many therapeutic uses. It can be used as an antiseptic and a local anesthetic.

### Pandan/pandanus leaf (Bai-Toey)

This has a distinctive and sweet scent and is often used in desserts and appetizers. The long, green leaves are perfect for wrapping marinated fish or meat while they are cooked. The green color that you often see in Thai desserts comes from squeezing the juice out of the leaves. The leaves are also used as one of the ingredients in a treatment for athlete's foot. Pandanus leaves are usually available in Asian foodstores and supermarkets, but if you can't find them, banana leaves or even foil can be used instead to wrap food in, although the taste will not be quite the same!

Pandanus leaves (*Bai-Toey*)

### Palm sugar (Nam-Taan-Peep)

This is made by boiling the nectar from the fruits of coconut palms, until it solidifies into a cake. Palm sugar has a very mild sweetness, unlike cane sugar, which is sharper. It is used in Thai cooking for both savory dishes and desserts.

### Fresh peppercorns (Med Prik-Tai-Oon)

These are often used in red curry paste-based dishes and are absolutely delicious when cooked. They look like small bunches of very tiny, dark green grapes. When dried, they turn into the more familiar black peppercorns. They help to reduce fever and aid digestion. The fresh bunches are sold in Thai foodstores, but they are also available in cans, which will need to be drained well before use. Within a few days of purchase, fresh peppercorns need to be kept in water so that they do not lose their freshness.

### Shrimp paste (Ga-Pi)

This is made from tiny shrimp. It has a muddy color and a very strong smell. Good *Ga-pi* should be quite moist, but firm. It is used in making a few types of chile-paste dips and in a few non-coconut-milk-based curries. You can substitute anchovy paste.

### Sour tamarind (Ma-Kham-Piak)

This usually comes dried in a compressed block, which needs to be soaked in warm water for about 10 minutes before the juice is squeezed out and strained through a strainer. The seeds and fibrous bits should be discarded, and the juice stored in the refrigerator until needed. This juice is often used in curries to give a gentle sourness. Lime or lemon juice can be used if you cannot find cooking tamarinds, but both tend to give a sharper sourness to the dish, so a small amount of sugar might be needed to tone this down. Look for blocks of tamarind in Asian foodstores, and small bottles of ready-to-use tamarind concentrate in supermarkets. Tamarind has long been one of the main ingredients that help eliminate constipation and it is believed to help lower high body temperature in the case of fever. You can also use sour tamarinds mixed with water to polish ornaments and cutlery made of brass or silver.

# Fruit and Vegetables

### Asparagus (Noa-Mai-Farang)

This vegetable is extremely popular in Thailand. Thais use asparagus in the same way that they use bamboo shoots to add crunch and texture to dishes. It is often used in quick stir-fries to give a nutty taste. Keep it in water as you would flowers in a vase. It has a similar texture to that of long beans, but is stringier. Asparagus stems are high in potassium and folic acid and a source of beta carotene and vitamin E. Asparagus can be used to treat rheumatism, gout, and cystitis.

### Cucumber (Tang-Goua)

Thai cucumbers are much smaller and paler in color and their seeds are less watery than those of the western cucumbers you find in your local supermarkets. They are tiny, crunchy, and extremely firm in texture. In this book, however, "cucumber" refers to western cucumbers. In Thailand cucumbers are eaten fresh with a chile dip, because they act as a cooling agent owing to their very high water content. They can be replaced with zucchini in stir-fries, mild soups, and vegetable selections served with chile dips. Because of their high water content they can be used to help relieve fever, thirst, and burns and also help to flush toxins out of the body. Thin slices of cucumber placed over the face help to hydrate and revitalize the skin. Cucumber leaves are also good for relieving stomach upsets. The bitter compound found in the leaves and stalks is believed to prevent cancer.

### Eggplant (Ma-Khue)

There are many varieties of these in Thailand, and each has a different use depending on the dish. For making chile dips, large ones are used. The small, round, pale green ones are commonly used in curries and often enjoyed as fresh vegetables with a dip. Baby eggplant that look like peas are also used in curries and in some chile dips. Obviously, if you can't find round eggplant, the larger, more widely available variety is an acceptable substitute. Eggplant contain calcium and iron, which is good for the blood. They are also extremely low in calories. Some varieties are used as a treatment for diabetes.

Thai eggplant (Ma-Khue-Proh)

### Green papaya (Ma-La-Gor Dib)

Green papaya is basically unripe papaya. In some dishes green papaya can be substituted with rutabaga, which has a similar texture. Green papaya is used in only a few—but very popular—Thai dishes. Unripe papaya contains high amounts of vitamins A and C and helps the process of digestion.

### Jelly/ear mushrooms (Hed-Hu-Noo)

This type of mushroom is usually available dried. The mushrooms grow on logs and tree trunks and are brownish black in color. Dried jelly mushrooms must be soaked in cold water for 30–45 minutes before cooking to return them to their original size and texture. They are very jelly-like, bouncy, and crunchy, yet have quite a sweet taste. Some people refer to them as "black fungus."

### Long/yard beans (Thua-Fak-Yao)

Long beans can be replaced with green beans. They do not keep fresh for as long as green beans but they are easier to prepare and cut. They can grow longer than 14 inches and are very popular in Thai cooking, used to give crunch and texture to many dishes. Stir-frying these beans with a few cloves of garlic and a dash of Thai fish sauce can make a great and simple dish. Long beans have a high concentration of vitamin C that promotes the absorption of iron needed to keep the blood healthy. They also help to reduce cholesterol.

### Morning glory (*Pauk-Boung*)

This is a favourite vegetable in Thailand—stir-fried morning glory with garlic and bird's eye chiles is as popular a dish as Thai Fried Omelet (page 82). There are two main types of morning glory: Water morning glory, which has large, fat leaves with both green and red tips and is used in stir-fries; and field morning glory, which has narrow leaves with red tips. Field morning glory is eaten with dips and eaten raw with Aromatic Spicy Green Papaya Salad (page 43). Morning glory is believed to soothe ulcers and is a good ingredient for diabetics who need to control their sugar intake. It is also an excellent source of vitamin A and iron.

### Shallots *(Hom Dang)*

These small onions are strong in taste and aroma. They are used in most spicy Thai salads. Crispy fried shallots are also used to make Thai baked custards (page 139). If you can't find shallots, red onions make a good substitute. Shallots are a useful agent in the alleviation of stomach discomfort and respiratory problems. They also help to relieve diarrhea and to relieve or prevent coughs.

### Straw mushrooms *(Hed-Hom)*

These mushrooms are grown in the north of Thailand where the weather is cooler. You usually find them in dried form. When dried, they are light in weight. To use, soak them in water for 30–45 minutes until they become quite meaty and chewy. They are used in mild soups with cucumber, and can be stir-fried with ginger and meat, or steamed with ginger and fish. They contain potassium, linoleic and folic acid, and iron and can be used to lower blood cholesterol. They stimulate the immune system and fight viral infections.

### White cabbage *(Pauk-Gad Khao)*

There are many types of cabbage. Thais use white cabbage in various dishes, such as soups, stir-fries, and as an accompaniment to salads or appetizers. White cabbage is high in vitamin C and can be used to ease pancreatic problems.

## Rice and Noodles

### Glass/transparent/cellophane noodles (*Woon-Sen*)

These are made from mung beans and are used in mild soups, salads, stir-fries, and steamed dishes. They come dried and must be soaked in water for about 2 hours before use.

### Thin rice noodles *(Guay-Tiew Sen-Lek)*

These can be fresh or dried. If dried, they must be soaked in water for about 2 hours to soften before use. They are about ⅛ inch wide and are used for stir-fried noodle dishes like Pad-Thai (page 122), noodle soups, and dry noodle dishes. They are very brittle when dry, so take care not to break them.

### Rice vermicelli *(Sen-Mee)*

Vermicelli usually come dried and must be soaked in water for about 2 hours to soften before use. They are the thinnest type of rice noodle and look like a thick piece of thread. They are used in a popular dish called Crispy Caramelized Noodles with Shrimp (page 125) and also for stir-fried noodle dishes, noodle soups, and dry noodle dishes.

### Wide rice noodles *(Guay-Tiew Sen-Yai)*

These are available fresh and dried. If dried, they must be soaked in water for about 2 hours to soften them before use. They are approximately ½ inch wide and are used in a stir-fried noodle dish called Stir-fried Wide Rice Noodles with Chicken and Vegetables (page 119). They can also be used for other stir-fried noodle dishes, noodle soups, and dry noodle dishes.

### Sticky rice *(Khao-Neow)*

Uncooked, this is more opaque than white rice. The grains are rounder in shape and white in color. Sticky rice will cook properly only if it has been soaked for at least 5 hours before steaming. Before steaming, wrap the grains in cheesecloth. The cooking time will vary with the quantity being cooked. Once cooked, the grains are quite transparent. For desserts, sticky rice is steamed in the same way, but is then transferred to a bowl containing a mixture of coconut milk and sugar: the rice must be added to the flavorings when it is hot. Stir everything together and cover with plastic wrap or a lid. The hot grains will absorb all the coconut milk mixture, resulting in a sweet, sticky rice.

### White rice (Khao-Jow)

This is a long-grain rice that is very fluffy once cooked. Jasmine rice is obtained by simply adding jasmine flower fragrance to the rice. Thais generally prefer to use old rice as it is easier to cook than newly harvested rice, which can become soggy once cooked. The rice needs to be rinsed well two or three times before cooking to remove all the starch and any dirt or small stones.

## How to choose the following ingredients:

### Eggs (Kai-Gai)

The shell should not be too shiny and should have tiny pores. Avoid eggs that have been scrubbed cleaned as this removes the shell's fibrous outer layer, which helps to slow down evaporation and preserves the egg. Eggs will last longer if they are kept cool. Use large eggs for all recipes.

### Crabs (Puu)

It is best to buy crabs when they are still alive. The male crab is more meaty than the female. You can spot the difference because female crabs have large breast plates and their shells echo when you tap them.

### Freshwater fish (Pla Naam Jeud)

Choose fish that have tight but not swollen flesh. They should have clear eyes, red gills, and transparent scales.

### Sea fish (Pla Naam Khem)

Make sure that the fish smells fresh; red gills and clear eyes are other indicators of freshness. The flesh should be tight and not swell when it is pressed. It is recommended that you freeze your fish once it has been gutted and cleaned if you are not using it at once.

### Mollusks (Hoi)

These should be bought when still alive. They are not easy to store, but if you don't want to use them immediately you should steam or boil them, let cool, remove them from their shells, and keep in the refrigerator for no more than 2 days.

### Shrimp (Goong)

Check that shrimp are firm and have transparent flesh.

Remember, the smaller the shrimp the tastier they will be. Lobsters are not very popular among the Thais, who find the flesh too tough, chewy, tasteless, and expensive!

### Squid (Pla-Muek)

Squid have a waxy skin, so once they are cleaned you should make a few slits in the flesh to allow seasoning to seep in. Fresh squid have a white, waxy appearance and are slippery to the touch. If squid smells at all, it has gone bad and should not be used. Squid tubes can be bought too—these should also be slippery and juicy, not dried out.

### Beef (Nuea Wua)

The most tender beef is from the neck and thighs of the animal and is suitable for boiling, steaming, stir-frying, and deep-frying. The chest and the stomach parts are used for stewing and curries. In almost all my recipes I recommend round of beef as it is nice and tender, but Thais love their beef with a bit of fat and tendon.

### Chicken (Gai)

Thais prefer dark meat, such as wings, thighs and legs with the skin left on, as these are tastier than white breast meat. However, all my recipes for stir-fries and curries use breast meat as this is what we use at the Busabong.

### Pork (Moo)

The loin is the most tender meat and is suitable for broiling; other parts of the pig are used for stir-frying and deep-frying.

### Beancurd (Tao-Hoo)

Beancurd comes in many types and forms, each of which is used for a different sort of cooking. Soft beancurd is added to mild soups and firm beancurd and beancurd cakes is used in stir-fries. Beancurd is easy to digest and does not need to be chewed that much, making it particularly suitable for the elderly who often don't have an efficient digestive system. It is very low in cholesterol and is therefore also great for people who are overweight or have high blood pressure. I am not a big fan of beancurd, and do not use it much in my recipes.

# Snacks and Soups

At the Busabong, we serve only the vegetarian version of this dish and it is probably the best-selling appetizer in the restaurant. I personally think this is because of the ingredients we use in the stuffing, which have a very clean taste. The common fillings for ordinary spring rolls are glass noodles, cabbage, straw mushrooms, bamboo shoots, and pork. However, I dislike bamboo shoots in any salads, crispy-fried, or steamed dishes as they have a very strong, unusual taste and smell. Strangely enough, they do go well in curry sauce and in any spicy stir-fried dishes.

# Vegan Sticks

Poa-Pia-Toaud Jae

20–25 spring roll wrappers, 4 x 4 inches each, thawed if frozen

flour paste, made by mixing 1 tablespoon all-purpose flour with 1 tablespoon water

vegetable oil, for deep-frying

*For the filling*

2 tablespoons sesame oil

1 peeled garlic clove pounded with 1 fresh cilantro root to make a paste

5½ oz white cabbage, cored and finely chopped

2¼ oz carrots, peeled and finely sliced into batons

8 black jelly mushrooms, soaked in cold water for 30–45 minutes until soft, then drained, and finely sliced

3 oz glass noodles, soaked in cold water for 2 hours, drained, and cut into 4-in lengths

1½ tablespoons light soy sauce

¼ teaspoon white pepper

1½ tablespoons white sugar

⅓ teaspoon salt

scant ¼ cup water

*For the Tangy Plum Sauce*

1 salted plum (see page 98), pit removed, and mashed

¾ cup white vinegar

½ cup white sugar

½ cup water

1 tablespoon shredded carrot

*Makes 20–25 sticks*

First make the Tangy Plum Sauce. Place the salted plum, vinegar, sugar and water in a small pan over low heat and stir until the sugar dissolves. Add the carrot and simmer, stirring, until the sauce thickens. Remove from the heat and let cool. This sauce keeps for a long time in a covered container in the refrigerator, but leave it to return to room temperature an hour before using so it isn't too sticky.

To make the filling, heat the sesame oil in a wok over low heat. Add the garlic and cilantro paste and stir-fry for 10 seconds. Add the vegetables and glass noodles and stir-fry until the vegetables begin to soften. Add all the remaining ingredients for the filling, and cook until they are well blended and the water has been absorbed. Transfer the mixture to a bowl and let cool: If the filling is hot when the Vegan Sticks are assembled, the wrappers will tear. (A few brands of wrapper are quite dry and easily torn, so it helps if you roll them when the filling is slightly warm, but good-quality wrappers can be rolled easily when the filling is cold. The wrappers require some flexibility as you need to roll them very tightly to prevent too much oil seeping in while they are deep-fried.)

Working with one spring roll wrapper at a time, place it on the counter with one corner pointing toward you. Place a heaped teaspoon of the noodle and vegetable mixture in the center, then fold the bottom corner over the filling. Tuck in both sides and roll to the end, using the flour paste to seal. Repeat until all the filling is used.

Heat enough oil for deep-frying in a wok over high heat until it reaches 350°F, or until a cube of bread browns in 30 seconds. Take care, as if the oil is too cold, the spring rolls will absorb too much oil, and if it is too hot, they will look burnt, but the filling will still be cold.

Working in batches, if necessary, deep-fry the Vegan Sticks until they are golden brown all over and float to the surface. Use a wire spoon or tongs to remove them from the oil and drain them well on paper towels.

Serve the Vegan Sticks immediately, with Tangy Plum Sauce on the side for dipping.

You can also make this dish with ground pork or chicken instead of the shrimp. You will find that drying the bread before spreading it with the shrimp topping will prevent too much oil from soaking in during the frying and make spreading the topping easier.

Shrimp toasts are not suitable for freezing. The shrimp paste will become quite dry, and if you deep-fry them from frozen, the bread will be over-crispy or burnt and the shrimp paste will be too dry by the time they have cooked through.

# Spiced Shrimp Toasts

Kha-Noum-Paung Naa-Goong

14 oz raw shrimp, peeled and deveined

1 egg, beaten

1 tablespoon Thai fish sauce

a pinch of ground white pepper

1 tablespoon very finely chopped peeled carrot

½ scallion, very finely chopped

1 peeled garlic clove pounded with ½ fresh cilantro root to make a paste

4 slices thick white bread that has been left to dry for around 2–3 hours

3¾–4 cups vegetable oil, for deep-frying

a few fresh cilantro leaves, to garnish

*For the Cucumber Relish*

1 cup white vinegar

½ cup water

3 tablespoons white sugar

1 teaspoon salt

½ medium cucumber, cut in 4 lengthwise, seeded, and finely sliced

4 shallots, thinly sliced

2 fresh red chiles, finely chopped into rounds

*Makes 32 bitesize pieces*

First begin to make the Cucumber Relish. Heat the vinegar and water in a small pan over low heat. Add the sugar and salt and stir until the sugar dissolves, then remove from the heat, and set aside to cool. When the mixture is cool, stir in the cucumber, shallots, and chiles.

While the relish is cooling, make the spicy shrimp topping. Put the shrimp in a food processor and process to make a thick paste. Transfer the paste to a bowl and stir in the beaten egg. Add the fish sauce, white pepper, carrot, scallion, and garlic and cilantro root paste and mix together with your hands, pressing and turning.

Divide the spiced shrimp paste equally among the bread slices, spreading it over the whole surface, including the crust.

Heat the oil in a deep, wide skillet or wok over medium heat until the temperature reaches about 350°F, or until a cube of bread browns within 30 seconds. If the oil is not hot enough before you add the bread, you will end up with very oily toasts.

Add as many slices of bread as will fit in the pan, shrimp side down, making sure the slices are covered with oil. Using tongs, flip the bread slices over, continually turning them backward and forward, until they are golden brown.

Use a pair of tongs to remove the toasts from the pan and cut each slice in half. Return the toasts to the hot oil and continue frying them in batches until the filling is cooked through and they are crispy on both sides.

Drain the toasts well on layers of folded paper towels, then cut each toast half into 4 pieces, and garnish with cilantro leaves. Serve immediately with the Cucumber Relish as a dip.

This dish is rarely found in Thailand nowadays as it is a very old recipe, but I think it is well worth reviving. You can also make this dish with ground pork or even very finely ground shrimp, but I prefer the softer texture that you get with chicken.

# Steamed Thai Dumplings

Kha-Noum-Jeeb Thai

*For the dumplings*

**2 peeled garlic cloves pounded with 2 fresh cilantro roots to make a paste**

**1 lb 2 oz canned water chestnuts, drained and very finely chopped**

**1 lb 4 oz chicken, very finely chopped or ground**

**4 tablespoons light soy sauce**

**2 tablespoons white sugar**

**½ teaspoon salt**

**1 teaspoon ground white pepper**

**about 50 wonton wrappers**

**Chiles in Vinegar (page 117), to serve**

*For the Sweet Soy Sauce*

**1 cup dark soy sauce**

**2¼ tablespoons white sugar**

**½ cup white vinegar**

**¼ teaspoon salt**

*For the Golden Fried Garlic*

**6 garlic cloves, peeled and lightly crushed**

**3 tablespoons vegetable oil**

*Makes about 50 dumplings*

Put all the ingredients for the dumplings, except the wonton wrappers, in a bowl and mix together with your hands, pressing and turning.

Working with one wonton wrapper at a time, place ½ tablespoon of the chicken filling in the center, then pull up the edges, and squeeze near the top to seal. Repeat until all the filling is used.

Lightly grease the steamer tray so the dumplings don't stick. Bring the water in the steamer to a boil, then lower the heat, and place the uncooked dumplings neatly on the greased tray. Return the water to a boil, cover the steamer, and cook for 20–30 minutes. If you have a large steamer, you should be able to cook all the dumplings at the same time using two or three layers of your steamer; if not, you will have to work in batches. To check if the dumplings are ready, cut one in half to see if the chicken is cooked through.

Meanwhile, make the Golden Fried Garlic by stir-frying the crushed garlic in the vegetable oil over low heat until it is golden brown. Once cool, it can be kept in an airtight container at room temperature for up to 3 months and used when needed. Make the Sweet Soy Sauce by stirring all the ingredients together until they are well blended.

To serve, drizzle some Sweet Soy Sauce over the cooked dumplings, then top with some Golden Fried Garlic with just a dash of its oil. The taste of the dumplings will be enhanced with a little Chiles in Vinegar, so serve this separately for people to help themselves.

You can cook a large batch of these dumplings and freeze them for later use. Once they are frozen, all you need to do is steam them again to heat them up. I don't advise you to reheat them in a microwave, as they will become too dry. However, if this is all you have, rest a saucer at the bottom of a bowl and pour in a small amount of water, making sure the water level is just below the saucer. Place the frozen dumplings on the saucer and cover the bowl. Heat on the defrost setting for about 5 minutes, then cook on a normal setting for another 2–3 minutes, checking regularly, until the filling is heated through.

These skewers are excellent served with steamed sticky rice and Aromatic Spicy Green Papaya Salad (page 43). They go extremely well together to make a simple, well-balanced meal.

These should be eaten as soon as they have been broiled, or the shrimp will become dry and chewy. It makes a real difference when you squeeze lemon juice over them before serving as this increases the intensity of their flavor. If you like, you can replace the shrimp with pieces of firm fish fillet, such as monkfish.

## Broiled Marinated Pork Skewers

Moo Ping

½ tablespoon coriander seeds

2 tablespoons all-purpose flour

½ tablespoon ground cumin

3 tablespoons Thai fish sauce

3 tablespoons vegetable oil

generous ¼ cup honey

2 peeled garlic cloves, pounded with 2 fresh cilantro roots to make a paste

2 teaspoon dark soy sauce

1 lb pork tenderloin, cut into long thin slices across the grain, about ⅛ inches in thickness

20–25 wooden skewers, 7½ inches long

North-Eastern-Style Chile Sauce (page 95), to serve

First, lightly toast the coriander seeds in a hot dry pan over low heat until they release their aroma, then coarsely pound them using a pestle and mortar. Make the pork marinade by putting the flour, ground coriander seeds, and ground cumin into a large bowl. Stir in the fish sauce, vegetable oil, honey, garlic and cilantro paste, and dark soy sauce.

Add the pork strips and mix until the seasoning is well distributed. Cover and chill for 1 hour.

Meanwhile, soak the skewers in cold water until you need to use them.

When they have finished marinating, thread the pork strips onto the skewers, and heat the broiler to high. Broil the skewers for about 5 minutes, turning them over halfway through cooking, until the pork is cooked through when you cut into one piece. Serve with North-Eastern-Style Chile Sauce on the side as a dip.

*Makes 20–25 skewers*

## Lemongrass Naked Shrimp

Goong Ping Ta-Krai

3 tablespoons vegetable oil

2 tablespoons ready-made red curry paste, stir-fried with oil and kaffir lime leaves (see page 15)

1 tablespoon freshly squeezed lemon juice

1 tablespoon Thai fish sauce

1 teaspoon white sugar

40 raw black jumbo shrimp, peeled and deveined, but with the tails left on

10 lemongrass stalks to use as skewers, sharpened at the top

6–8 lemon wedges, to serve

Combine the vegetable oil, red curry paste, lemon juice, fish sauce, and sugar in a large, nonmetallic bowl. Add the shrimp, stirring so they are well coated, and then cover with plastic wrap and place in the refrigerator to marinate for 15 minutes.

Preheat the broiler to high. Thread 4 shrimp onto each lemongrass stalk. Place under the hot broiler for about 3 minutes, turning the lemongrass stalks occasionally, until the shrimp have cooked through and become opaque.

*Makes 10 skewers*

These are ideal for entertaining, as they can be assembled and frozen, ready for deep-frying straight from the freezer. They are very similar to Crispy Butterfly Shrimp, which are shrimp that have been coated with a light batter. However, Jacketed Shrimp are less messy and can be kept in a freezer ready to be deep-fried whenever you need them.

I like to make my own Sweet Chile and Garlic Sauce to serve with these delicious scallops, but, if you want to save time, you can buy it in most supermarkets, as well as Asian foodstores. Look for it in bottles labeled as *Naam Jim Gai*. In this recipe the scallops can be replaced with monkfish fillet cubes, or beancurd cubes for a vegetarian option; pineapple cubes, cherry tomatoes, or green bell pepper can be used instead of the red bell pepper.

# Jacketed Shrimp

Goong Hom Sa-Bai

2 peeled garlic cloves pounded with 2 fresh cilantro roots to make a paste

1 tablespoon Thai fish sauce

1 teaspoon white sugar

24 raw black jumbo shrimp, peeled and deveined but with the tails left on

24 spring roll wrappers, 4 x 4 inches each, thawed if frozen

flour paste, made by mixing 1 tablespoon all-purpose flour with 1 tablespoon water

vegetable oil, for deep-frying

Tangy Plum Sauce (page 22), to serve

*Makes 24*

Combine the garlic and cilantro paste, fish sauce, and white sugar together. Add the shrimp and stir until they are well coated.

Working with one spring roll wrapper at a time, place it on the counter with one corner pointing toward you. Fold over the right-hand corner to a depth of about 1 inch. Place a shrimp horizontally in the center of the wrapper, with the tail hanging out over the folded side. Fold the bottom corner over the shrimp and then fold the other two sides of the wrapper over to seal the shrimp tightly in the wrapper, using the flour paste to seal it. Continue until all the shrimp have been wrapped.

Heat enough oil for deep-frying in a wok over high heat until it reaches 350°F, or until a cube of bread browns in 30 seconds. Working in batches, if necessary, deep-fry the shrimp until they are golden brown all over and float to the surface. Use a wire spoon or tongs to remove them from the oil and drain them well on paper towels.

Serve hot with Tangy Plum Sauce for dipping.

# Broiled Spiced Scallops

Hoi-Shell Ping

2 peeled garlic cloves pounded with 2 fresh cilantro roots to make a paste

⅔ cup coconut cream

2 tablespoons Thai fish sauce

½ teaspoon ground cumin

½ teaspoon ground coriander

¼ teaspoon white pepper

1 lb 2 oz shelled fresh scallops

2 large red bell peppers, cored, seeded, and cut into 1-inch pieces

8–10 wooden skewers, 7½ inches long

a few fresh cilantro leaves, to garnish

*For the Sweet Chile and Garlic Sauce*

6 fresh red chiles, seeds removed from 3, finely chopped

6 garlic cloves

½ cup white vinegar

½ cup sugar

1 teaspoon salt

*Makes 8–10 skewers*

First, make the Sweet Chile and Garlic Sauce. Process the chiles and garlic in a small food processor, or use a pestle and mortar, until a paste forms. Heat the vinegar in a pan over low heat, and stir in the sugar and salt until dissolved. Add the chile and garlic paste and simmer, stirring occasionally, until the sauce thickens. Set aside to cool. The sauce can be kept in the refrigerator for up to 3 months and used as needed.

Combine the garlic and cilantro paste with the coconut cream and fish sauce in a large bowl. Gently stir in the cumin, coriander, and pepper until well blended. Add the scallops, stirring to coat them, then cover and place in the refrigerator to marinate for about 20 minutes.

Soak the skewers in cold water.

When you are ready to cook, preheat the broiler to high. Thread 3 or 4 scallops onto each skewer, alternating with pieces of red bell pepper. Broil for about 2 minutes, turning halfway through cooking, until the scallops are opaque.

Serve hot, drizzled with Sweet Chile and Garlic Sauce and garnished with cilantro leaves.

At my restaurant I serve these satay skewers with a few pieces of toast to mop up any peanut sauce left on the plate. The sauce is so good you don't want to leave any of it behind! It is also great served as a dip with shrimp or rice crackers. For variety, you can replace the chicken with pork, beef, or shrimp. Just remember shrimp take less time to marinate and cook and do not need to be tenderized.

# Chicken Satay

Gai Sateh

1 teaspoon coriander seeds

1 tablespoon finely chopped lemongrass

2 teaspoon ground turmeric

1 teaspoon ground cumin

2 tablespoons white sugar

2 teaspoon salt

6 tablespoons vegetable oil

⅔ cup coconut cream

2 lb chicken breast fillet, sliced lengthwise along the grain into 4 x 1-inch slices

25–30 wooden skewers, 7½ inches long

Cucumber Relish (page 23), to serve

*For the Curried Peanut Sauce*

1 tablespoon vegetable oil

1¾ cups canned coconut milk, unshaken

1½ tablespoons ready-made red curry paste

2 cups salted roasted peanuts, coarsely crushed

½ cup white sugar

½ teaspoon salt

6 kaffir lime leaves, torn

*Makes 25–30 skewers*

First toast the coriander seeds by tossing them in a dry pan over low heat until they are slightly browned and release an aroma.

Next pound the lemongrass, ground turmeric, and coriander seeds using a pestle and mortar. Add the remaining ingredients, except the coconut cream and chicken.

Add the chicken strips, using your hand to mix them well with the marinade, then cover, and set aside to marinate for 1 hour.

While the chicken is marinating, soak the wooden skewers in cold water.

Meanwhile, make the Curried Peanut Sauce. Heat the vegetable oil in a pan and stir-fry the red curry paste with the kaffir lime leaves for 1 minute. Place 3 tablespoons of the coconut cream (the thick part floating on top in the can) in a pan over a medium heat. Stir in the crushed peanuts and continue stirring until the mixture thickens. Stir in the remaining coconut milk, the sugar, and salt and continue simmering until thick. Remove from the heat and let cool.

When you are ready to cook, preheat the broiler to high. Thread the chicken strips onto the skewers, then brush the chicken with the coconut cream. If you don't have a suitable pastry brush, put the coconut cream in a tall, thin jar and dip the skewers in before broiling.

Place the skewers under the broiler and broil for about 4 minutes, turning halfway through cooking, or until the chicken is cooked through and the juices run clear when you pierce a piece with a knife.

Serve immediately with the Curried Peanut Sauce and Cucumber Relish.

Corn cakes were added to the Busabong menu only about 4 years ago. I decided to include them because the Thai fish cakes were so popular and so many requests came from our regular customers who were vegetarian. As the method for making both types is very similar, I've also given you a fishy alternative below.

# Spicy Corn Cakes

Toaud-Man Khao-Poud

**6 cups canned corn, drained**

**2 tablespoons ready-made red curry paste, stir-fried with oil and kaffir lime leaves (see page 60)**

**4 teaspoons white sugar**

**1 teaspoon salt**

**6 kaffir lime leaves, finely chopped**

**¼ cup tapioca flour**

**vegetable oil, for deep-frying**

*For the Chile and Peanut Dip*

**1 cup Sweet Chilli and Garlic Sauce (page 28)**

**¼ cup seeded and finely chopped cucumber**

**2½ tablespoons finely chopped carrot**

**1½ tablespoons salted roasted peanuts, crushed**

**1 tablespoon white vinegar**

*Makes 25–30 cakes*

To make the Chile and Peanut Dip, put all the ingredients in a bowl and stir together until blended, then set aside.

To make the corn cakes, put the corn, red curry paste, sugar, and salt in a food processor and process until a thick paste forms. Transfer the paste to a bowl and stir in the kaffir lime leaves and tapioca flour.

Lightly oil your fingertips and roll a tablespoonful of corn paste into a ball, then flatten it by pressing. Set aside the corn cake and continue until all the mixture is used.

Heat enough oil for deep-frying in a wok over high heat until it reaches 350°F, or until a cube of bread browns in 30 seconds. Working in batches, if necessary, deep-fry the corn cakes, turning them often, until they are golden brown all over and float to the surface. Use a wire spoon or tongs to remove them from the oil and drain them well on paper towels. Continue until all the corn cakes are fried.

Serve the corn cakes immediately with the Chile and Peanut Dip on the side.

Alternatively, you can make fish cakes by replacing the corn with cod or monkfish fillet (a better choice, but more expensive), or you can mix together both fish to give your cakes a more chewy texture. If you are using fish rather than corn, use 2½ tablespoons fish sauce instead of salt, add a few finely chopped green beans, double the amount of red curry paste, and omit the tapioca flour. Double the blending time in the food processor. (Frozen fish paste, specifically produced for Thai fish cakes, is also available in Asian supermarkets. It is called "grey feather fish paste.")

Corn cakes cannot be frozen for future use because they do not have a firm texture. Fish cakes, however, can be frozen once they have been half deep-fried to keep their shape. Thaw completely before deep-frying again for a few minutes to finish the cooking.

Another well-known name for this dish is "Chicken Wrapped in Leaves." I decided to call it Pyramid Chicken because it really looks like a pyramid if properly wrapped. The larger the pandanus leaf, the better the chicken will taste and smell. This is because a large leaf can be wrapped around the chicken piece in two or three layers to protect the meat, insuring it stays moist and tender while the inside is cooked. The pandanus leaf will also transfer its sweet and smoky flavor to the chicken during cooking. You can substitute fish fillets for chicken, if you like, but remember that fish takes less time to cook.

# Aromatic Pyramid Chicken

Gai Hoa Bai-Toey

**1 lb skinless, boneless chicken breast portion, cut into ¾ inch cubes**

**2 tablespoons sesame oil**

**1½ tablespoons white sugar**

**3 tablespoons light soy sauce**

**½ tablespoon salt**

**2 tablespoons smooth chile sauce (optional)**

**20–25 pandanus leaves**

**vegetable oil, for deep-frying**

*For the Light Soy Sauce with Sesame Oil*

**½ cup light soy sauce**

**1 tablespoon white sugar**

**1 tablespoon sesame oil**

**1 teaspoon sesame seeds (optional)**

*Makes 20–25 pieces*

Put the chicken, sesame oil, sugar, soy sauce, salt, and chile sauce, if using, into a bowl and mix together well. Set aside and leave to marinate for 1 hour.

Wash and wipe dry the pandanus leaves.

Make the Light Soy Sauce with Sesame Oil by stirring together the soy sauce, sugar, and oil in a small bowl. To give the sesame seeds extra punch, toast them in a dry wok or skillet over low heat just until they turn golden brown. Immediately tip them out of the pan, then add them to the other ingredients, and set aside.

Wrap each chicken piece in a piece of pandanus leaf, making a triangle shape. Secure the parcel closed with a wooden toothpick and set aside while you continue making parcels until all the chicken pieces are used.

Heat enough oil for deep-frying in a wok over high heat until it reaches 350°F, or until a cube of bread browns in 30 seconds. Working in batches, if necessary, deep-fry the chicken parcels, turning them often, for about 4 minutes until they float to the surface and the juices run clear when you cut into one. Use a wire spoon or tongs to remove them from the oil and drain them well on paper towels. Continue until all the chicken parcels are deep-fried.

You can serve the chicken with or without the leaf wrapping with the Light Soy Sauce with Sesame Oil for dipping. The leaves can be chewy so you might want to remove them. As the sweet aroma from the leaf transfers to the chicken while it is being cooked, it is not necessary to eat the leaf.

This is an infinitely versatile recipe. For a vegetarian version, use vegetable stock or water (see tips in the main Introduction). The pork and shrimp can also be replaced with thinly sliced vegetables such as scallions, cucumber, and squash.

# Glass Noodle Soup with Shrimp and Pork Balls

Tom-Jued Woon-Sen Moo-Saub

¼ cup ground pork

1 peeled garlic clove pounded with 1 fresh cilantro root to make a paste

1½ cups chicken stock or water

1 cilantro root, lightly pounded

1 peeled garlic clove, lightly pounded

1 tablespoon cooked shrimp

1 oz onion, thinly sliced

4 black jelly mushrooms, soaked in cold water for 30–45 minutes until soft, then drained

1 oz glass noodles, soaked in cold water for 1–2 hours and drained well

1 scallion, thinly sliced lengthwise

2½ tablespoons Thai fish sauce

¾ teaspoon sugar

*For the garnish*

1 teaspoon Golden Fried Garlic (page 25)

a few fresh cilantro leaves

freshly ground black pepper

*Serves 4 as part of a main meal or 2 as an appetizer*

In a large bowl combine the pork and garlic and coriander paste and shape it into small balls, around 1 inch in diameter.

Bring the stock or water to a boil, then add the pounded cilantro and garlic, and simmer for a few minutes to release its aroma. Add the pork balls to the boiling stock and cook for about 2–3 minutes, or until the pork is cooked, skimming the surface as necessary. Lots of tiny bubbles will form when you add the pork balls to the soup and it is important to remove as many as possible to keep the soup crystal clear.

Reduce the heat and stir in the shrimp, followed by the sliced onion, mushrooms, noodles, scallion, fish sauce, and sugar. Continue simmering for 1 minute more, then ladle into individual bowls. Serve garnished with fried garlic, cilantro leaves, and a grind of black pepper.

Roasted chile paste is sold in Thai foodstores and in most supermarkets. Most brands include dried shrimp, so omit it when you are making a vegetarian dish, or look for a vegetarian version. You can replace the shrimp with chicken, fish, or seafood, but remember that it takes slightly longer to cook chicken. Some people like to use shrimp shells to make stock for this soup, but you must use only a very small quantity or the smell of the stock will overpower the wonderful aroma from the herbs.

# Lemongrass Soup with Shrimp and Oyster Mushrooms

Tom-Yum Goong

3 cups chicken stock

2 cilantro roots, lightly crushed

4 kaffir lime leaves

2 lemongrass stalks, lightly crushed

2 inches galangal, lightly crushed

4½ tablespoons Thai fish sauce

2 teaspoons white sugar

3½ oz medium raw black jumbo shrimp, peeled and deveined

2 oz oyster mushrooms, trimmed if necessary

2 bird's eye chiles, lightly crushed

4 tablespoons freshly squeezed lemon juice or 3½ tablespoons freshly squeezed lime juice

1 teaspoon roasted chile paste (optional)

a few fresh cilantro leaves, to garnish

*Serves 4 as part of a main meal, or 2 as an appetizer*

Bring the stock to a boil in a wok or pan over high heat. Reduce the heat to low, add the cilantro roots, kaffir lime leaves, lemongrass, and galangal, and continue simmering for about 10 minutes, until the herbs have released their aroma.

Stir in the fish sauce and sugar, then add the shrimp and mushrooms, turn up the heat, and continue simmering until the shrimp are just cooked through and turn opaque. Turn off the heat and stir in the chiles, then add the lemon or lime juice. This should always be added last as cooked lemon juice can taste unpleasant, while fresh juice tastes sharp and pungent, and retains its citrus aroma.

Transfer the soup to a bowl, then stir in the roasted chile paste, if using, and sprinkle with cilantro leaves.

I prefer to flavor this soup with salt, rather than the more usual fish sauce, as it does not darken the color of the coconut milk. For a vegetarian version, the chicken stock can be replaced with water or vegetable stock, and you can increase the amount of oyster mushrooms to replace the chicken. Also, don't forget that most Thai roasted chile paste contains dried shrimp, so be sure to look for a vegetarian one, or leave it out all together.

# Herbal Spicy Lemongrass Soup with Coconut Milk and Galangal

Tom-Kha Gai

1¾ cups canned coconut milk, well shaken

2 lemongrass stalks, lightly crushed

2 fresh cilantro roots, lightly crushed

4 kaffir lime leaves, torn

2 inches galangal, thinly sliced

1 cup chicken stock or water

1 teaspoon salt or 3½ tablespoons Thai fish sauce

2 teaspoons white sugar

10 oz skinless, boneless chicken breast portions, cut into thin slices along the grain

2 oz wild or oyster mushrooms, trimmed if necessary

2 bird's eye chiles, lightly crushed

3 tablespoons freshly squeezed lemon juice or 2½ tablespoons freshly squeezed lime juice

1 teaspoon roasted chile paste (optional)

*For the garnish*

2 dried roasted chiles, chopped

a few fresh cilantro leaves

*Serves 4 as part of a main meal or 2 as an appetizer*

Put the coconut milk in a pan over high heat and bring to a boil. Add the lemongrass stalks, cilantro roots, lime leaves, and galangal, reduce the heat to low, add the stock or water, and simmer for 10 minutes.

Season the soup with the salt or fish sauce and sugar and stir well. Add the chicken, turn up the heat, and continue simmering for about 2–3 minutes, until the chicken is cooked through and the juices run clear when you cut into one piece.

Stir in the mushrooms and cook for a minute or so, then turn off the heat, and add the chiles and lemon or lime juice. Transfer the soup into a serving bowl and stir in the roasted chile paste, if using. Serve garnished with dried roasted chiles and a few cilantro leaves.

This soup really reminds me of my childhood. My grandmother used to make it for me before I developed a taste for spicy food. I used to put a few scoops of boiled rice into the soup and eat it just like that! Not quite my grandmother's idea of good behavior—I was told off quite often for doing it. I still do it, though, but only when I'm with my young son, Timothy, as he does the same to his *Tom-Yum* soup. Sliced chicken, ground pork balls, or shrimp can be added to the stock with the cucumbers and scallions for a more filling soup.

# Clear and Mild Soup with Cucumber and Scallions

Tom-Jued Tang-Goua

1¼ cups vegetable stock or water

1 fresh cilantro root, lightly pounded

1½ cups seeded and coarsely chopped cucumber

3 tablespoons peeled and coarsely chopped onion

4½ teaspoons Thai fish sauce, or salt to taste for vegetarians

1½ teaspoons sugar

2 scallions, cut into 1-inch lengths

1 teaspoon Golden Fried Garlic (page 25)

*For the garnish*

a few fresh cilantro leaves

a pinch of ground black pepper

*Serves 4 as part of a main meal or 2 as an appetizer*

Place the stock or water in a pan over high heat and bring to a boil. Add the cilantro root, reduce the heat to low, and simmer for 10 minutes.

Increase the heat to medium, and add the cucumber and chopped onion. Season the soup with the fish sauce or salt and sugar, stir well, and simmer for about 3 minutes.

Stir in the scallions, then transfer the soup to a serving bowl. Sprinkle with the Golden Fried Garlic, and garnish with cilantro leaves and a sprinkling of pepper.

# Salads

The main aroma of this salad comes from the ground toasted rice, and without it the dish could not be called *larb*. Although sticky rice is authentic, ordinary white long-grain rice can also be used, and ground chicken or beef can be used instead of the pork.

# North-Eastern Thai Salad with Pork

Larb Moo

1⅓ cups ground pork

1½ tablespoons uncooked sticky rice

½ teaspoon white sugar

1½ tablespoons Thai fish sauce

3 shallots, peeled and finely chopped

1 scallion, finely chopped

a few fresh mint leaves

¼ teaspoon Bird's Eye Chile Powder (page 95)

2¼ tablespoons freshly squeezed lemon juice, or 1½ tablespoons freshly squeezed lime juice

2 tablespoons chicken stock or water, boiled and cooled (optional)

a few fresh cilantro leaves, to garnish

*To serve*

a few raw green or long beans, trimmed

some white cabbage, coarsely sliced

*Serves 4 as part of a meal*

Bring a pan of water to a boil over medium heat. Add the pork and boil for about 2½ minutes, stirring to break it up, until it loses all its pinkness. Drain the pork well and set aside.

Heat a dry wok or skillet over high heat. Reduce the heat to low, add the rice grains, and stir them around until they turn golden brown. Immediately tip the rice out of the pan, then use a pestle and mortar to pound into tiny grains.

Add the rice to the cooked pork, then add the sugar and fish sauce, and toss them all together. Add the shallots, scallion, half of the mint leaves, the Bird's Eye Chile Powder, and lemon or lime juice and toss again. Only add the chicken stock or water if the salad seems too dry.

Transfer the salad to a plate, garnish with the cilantro leaves, and serve with the remaining mint leaves, the beans, and cabbage on the side.

This is such a common salad in Thailand that it was impossible to leave it out of this book. It is particularly popular with people who are on a diet! Although my preference would be to make it with salted field crabs, they are not widely available, so I have used more common ingredients. I'm not keen on the texture of sun-dried shrimp, so for a non-vegetarian version, I use small shrimp that have been deep-fried for a few seconds to make them drier.

# Aromatic Spicy Green Papaya Salad

Som-Tam Jae

4–5 long or green beans, cut into 1-inch lengths

1 garlic clove, peeled and crushed

1 fresh bird's eye chile

2½ oz green papaya, peeled, seeded, and shredded

1 medium tomato, cut into wedges

1¼ teaspoons white sugar or 1½ teaspoons palm sugar

1½ tablespoons freshly squeezed lemon juice or 1 tablespoon freshly squeezed lime juice

1 tablespoon Thai fish sauce, or ¼ teaspoon salt for vegetarians

*To serve*

a few morning glories, cut about 5 inches from the tips

some white cabbage, coarsely sliced

a few raw long beans, cut into 3-inch lengths

*Serves 4 as part of a meal*

To make the dressing, use a pestle and mortar to crush the garlic and chile. Add the beans and lightly pound. Next add the papaya and tomato pieces and keep pounding lightly. The idea is to just break open the green papaya so it absorbs all the dressing ingredients. If you have a stone pestle and mortar, be very gentle when you are pounding the ingredients; a wooden pestle and mortar are better.

Sprinkle over the sugar, lemon or lime juice, and fish sauce or salt, then use a spoon to keep turning over and tossing all the ingredients until well mixed. If you are using palm sugar, make sure that any lumps are broken up.

Serve the salad with morning glories, white cabbage, and green beans on the side.

The inspiration for this dish came from visiting an Italian restaurant one evening with a friend in Bangkok. Olive oil and balsamic vinegar are replaced by fresh chiles, garlic, orange juice, and lemon juice, meaning that the only oil in the salad comes from the soft-shell crabs. Orange juice makes such a difference to the salad, as it adds tangy flavor, citrus aroma, and natural sweetness. It's a great combination that can be eaten by itself as a light lunch.

## Tangy Soft-shell Crab Salad

Sa-Lad Puu-Nim

1 cup all-purpose flour

scant ½ cup water

2 prime-sized soft-shell crabs, each weighing around 3 oz

vegetable oil, for deep-frying

3½ oz mixed salad greens, including arugula

6 cherry tomatoes, cut in half

3 tablespoons shredded carrot

*For the dressing*

freshly squeezed juice of ½ orange

flesh of ½ orange, finely chopped

1 teaspoon sugar

1 fresh bird's eye chile, lightly crushed

1 garlic clove, peeled and crushed

1½ tablespoons Thai fish sauce

2¼ tablespoons freshly squeezed lemon juice, or 1½ tablespoons freshly squeezed lime juice

*Serves 4 as part of a meal or 1 individually*

Put ¾ cup of the flour in a large bowl and stir in the water to make a smooth paste. Add the crabs to the bowl and coat them with the flour paste, then lift each crab, and let the excess paste drip off. Lightly sprinkle each crab with the remaining dry flour to hold the paste in place on the shiny, slippery shells.

Heat enough oil for deep-frying in a wok over high heat until it reaches 350°F, or until a cube of bread browns in 30 seconds. Add the crabs and deep-fry for about 2 minutes until crisp and golden brown all over. Use a wire spoon or tongs to remove the crabs from the oil and drain them well on paper towels.

Make the dressing by whisking all the ingredients together in a bowl. Stir the cherry tomatoes and the shredded carrot into the dressing. Put the salad greens in a serving bowl, add the dressed tomatoes and carrot and any remaining dressing, and gently toss together.

Cut the crabs in half and arrange the pieces over the dressed salad.

This is a lovely and healthy dish. Glass noodles are made from mung beans or green beans and are a great source of protein, unlike rice noodles. They also contain a huge amount of water which fills you up when you eat them, making this salad very popular among those on a diet. You should avoid eating glass noodles at bedtime as they tend to expand in your stomach, like Steamed Sticky Rice (page 106)! If you are a vegetarian, just replace the chicken and shrimp with more glass noodles and mushrooms.

# Glass Noodle and Jelly Mushroom Salad

Yum Woon-Sen

2 oz glass noodles, soaked in cold water for 2 hours, and drained well

¼ cup ground chicken

1 tablespoon cooked shrimp

4–5 dried black jelly mushrooms, soaked in cold water for 30–45 minutes, then drained and coarsely sliced

2 tablespoons peeled, grated carrot

1 oz oyster mushrooms, trimmed, if necessary, and torn by hand

2 shallots, or ¼ red onion, peeled and thinly sliced

2 teaspoons thinly sliced celery (optional)

*For the dressing*

2¼ tablespoons freshly squeezed lemon juice or 1½ tablespoons freshly squeezed lime juice

1½ tablespoons Thai fish sauce or ⅓ teaspoon salt

1 garlic clove, peeled and finely crushed

1 fresh bird's eye chile, lightly crushed

1 teaspoon white sugar

½ scallion, finely chopped

*For the garnish*

1 teaspoon Golden Fried Garlic (page 25)

a few fresh cilantro leaves

*Serves 4 as part of a meal or 1 individually*

Cut the noodles into 6-inch lengths. Set aside.

Bring a pan of water to a boil, then add the chicken, and cook for about 2 minutes until only half cooked. Add the shrimp, glass noodles, and jelly mushrooms.

When the glass noodles turn clear and the chicken is cooked through, drain well and transfer the ingredients to a bowl. Be careful not to over-cook the glass noodles as if they absorb too much water they won't be able to soak up any of the dressing. They usually take less than a minute to become tender.

Add the carrot, mushrooms, shallots or red onion, and celery, if using, and gently toss together.

To make the dressing, combine the lemon or lime juice, fish sauce or salt, the garlic, chile, sugar, and scallion. Add the dressing to the salad and again gently toss, taking care not to break up the noodles too much. Serve sprinkled with the Golden Fried Garlic and cilantro leaves.

Cook the beef in advance so it has plenty of time to cool; if it is added to the other ingredients while still hot, it will "cook" the vegetables and they will lose their crispness.

Leaving the skin on the duck breast makes it nice and crispy when it is deep-fried, adding an extra texture to this fresh and crunchy salad.

## Broiled Beef Salad
Yum Nuea

## Crispy Duck Salad
Sa-lad Ped-Grob

**7 oz beef round, in one piece**

**2 fresh bird's eye chiles**

**1 garlic clove, peeled and coarsely chopped**

**1½ tablespoons Thai fish sauce**

**2¼ tablespoons freshly squeezed lemon juice**

**1 teaspoon white sugar**

**1¼ oz cucumber, finely sliced**

**1 tomato, cut into wedges**

**1 tablespoon thinly sliced peeled, onion**

**1 scallion, chopped**

**a few fresh cilantro leaves, to garnish**

*Serves 4 as part of a meal or 1 individually*

Preheat the broiler to medium-high and lightly grease the broiler rack. Place the beef on the rack and broil for 2–3 minutes on each side until it is medium-rare, then set aside to cool.

Pound the chiles and garlic together using a pestle and mortar until a paste forms. Transfer to a large bowl and stir in the fish sauce, lemon juice, and sugar.

Thinly slice the beef and add it to the bowl, along with the cucumber, tomato, onion, and scallion and very gently toss together. Transfer the salad to a plate and garnish with cilantro leaves.

**4 oz roasted boneless duck breast, with the skin on, thinly sliced**

**1 cup all-purpose flour**

**vegetable oil, for deep-frying**

**4½ oz white cabbage, cored and thinly sliced**

**1½ oz carrot, peeled and cut into thin batons**

**2 garlic cloves, peeled and crushed**

**2 fresh bird's eye chiles, lightly crushed**

**1½ teaspoon white sugar**

**2 tablespoons Thai fish sauce**

**3 tablespoons freshly squeezed lemon juice or 2¼ tablespoons freshly squeezed lime juice**

**a few fresh cilantro leaves, to garnish**

*Serves 4 as part of a meal or 1 individually*

Sprinkle the duck slices with a little water, then coat them with the flour, shaking off any excess. (Lightly wetting the duck slices with water before they are fried helps the dry flour to stick.) Do not, however, add the water to the flour as you don't want a thick coating.

Heat enough oil for deep-frying in a wok over high heat until it reaches 350°F, or until a cube of bread browns in 30 seconds. Add the duck slices and deep-fry for 1–2 minutes, stirring the slices around, until they become golden brown and crisp. Use a wire spoon or tongs to remove the duck slices from the oil and drain them well on paper towels.

Combine the cabbage and carrot in a bowl, then add the garlic, chiles, sugar, fish sauce, and lemon juice or lime juice, and toss together again until well mixed.

Transfer the salad to a bowl and sprinkle the crispy duck on top, then sprinkle with the cilantro leaves.

This crisp, crunchy salad tastes best when the peanut sauce is warm, but not so hot that it wilts the vegetables. If you want to make a real meal out of this salad, add deep-fried beancurd cubes along with bean sprouts.

Salmon fillet also works well in this salad. Just be careful not to overcook the fish. It has the best texture when it is medium-rare.

# Mixed Salad with Curried Peanut Sauce

Sa-Lad Khaek

# Spicy Tuna Salad with Lemongrass

Yum Pla-Tuna Soung-Kriong

½ medium lettuce, broken into leaves, or any mixed salad greens of your choice, rinsed and dried

1 hard-cooked egg, shelled and cut into slices or wedges, as you like

10 thin cucumber slices, halved

10 thin tomato slices, halved

½ onion, peeled and sliced into rings

3 tablespoons shredded carrot

4 tablespoons Curried Peanut Sauce (page 29), warmed

a few fresh cilantro leaves, to garnish

skin of 1 tomato, shaped into a rose (optional)

*Serves 4 as part of a meal, or 1 individually*

Arrange the lettuce or salad greens on a large platter. Arrange the hard-cooked egg and the cucumber, tomato, and onion slices on top of the lettuce and sprinkle the shredded carrot and cucumber over them. Drizzle the warmed Curried Peanut Sauce over the top and garnish with a few cilantro leaves and the tomato rose, if using.

1 tuna steak, 9–10½ oz

1 garlic clove, peeled and coarsely chopped

2 fresh bird's eye chiles

1½ tablespoons Thai fish sauce

1 teaspoon white sugar

1 scallion, finely chopped

1 oz thinly sliced peeled onion

3 tablespoons shredded carrot

1 tablespoon thinly sliced lemongrass

2¼ tablespoons freshly squeezed lemon juice or 1½ tablespoons freshly squeezed lime juice

a few fresh cilantro leaves, to garnish

*Serves 4 as part of a meal or 1 individually*

Preheat the broiler to medium-high and lightly grease the broiler rack. Place the tuna steak on the rack and broil for about 2 minutes on each side until medium-rare (the outside is sealed, but the inside is still a little raw), then set aside to cool.

Use a pestle and mortar to pound the garlic and chile together, then transfer to a large bowl. Stir in the fish sauce and sugar.

Slice the tuna steak into thin pieces and toss well in the dressing, Add the scallion, onion, carrot, lemongrass, and lemon or lime juice and gently toss one more time.

Transfer the salad to a serving bowl or plates and garnish with cilantro leaves.

You can buy bags of ready-fried shallots in Thai foodstores, but it takes very little effort to make your own. Make more than you need, as they keep for weeks in a covered container in the refrigerator.

They are usually added to the dish at the last moment before serving so that they stay crisp. Don't use green cooking apples for this salad, as they tend to be too sour.

# Aromatic Apple Salad with Crispy Rice Cakes

Yum Ab-Peon

1 tablespoon Thai fish sauce, or ⅓ teaspoon salt for vegetarians

1 fresh bird's eye chile, pounded

1 garlic clove, peeled and crushed

1 teaspoon white sugar

1 red apple, cored and chopped into small cubes

1 green apple, cored and chopped into small cubes

3 tablespoons shredded carrot

1½ tablespoons freshly squeezed lemon juice, or 1 tablespoon freshly squeezed lime juice

4–5 salted or unsalted rice crackers, as desired, per person, to serve

*For the Fried Shallots*

2 shallots, peeled and thinly sliced

2 tablespoons vegetable oil

*Serves 4 as part of a meal or 1 individually*

First make a batch of Fried Shallots. Heat the oil in a wok over medium heat. Add the shallot slices and deep-fry, stirring, until they turn golden brown and crisp. Use a wire spoon to remove them from the oil and drain them well on paper towels.

Combine the fish sauce, chile, garlic, and sugar in a bowl, stirring until the sugar dissolves.

Stir in the red and green apples, the carrot, lemon or lime juice, and 1 teaspoon of the Fried Shallots and toss together. Transfer to a large plate or bowl and serve with rice crackers on the side.

As I have mentioned, Thais like meat or poultry with the skin on and also on the bone as we think this makes a dish taste much better and juicier. Breast portions are too dry for the Thais, but very popular in the West. When we prepare chicken to be used at the restaurant, we separate the white meat, the dark meat, and the skin. The white meat is used in all the dishes prepared for the customers, the dark meat gets ground and is used to make stuffing. The skin isn't wasted: We cut it into smaller pieces and deep-fry them so they are nice and crispy. As deep-fried chicken skin is quite fattening and could taste overpowering if eaten on its own, we add herbs and vegetables to give a lighter and more fragrant taste to this dish.

# Crispy Chicken Skin Salad

Yum Nang-Gai Toaud

**vegetable oil, for deep-frying**

**4½ oz chicken skin, plucked, cleaned, and cut into small pieces**

**2 fresh bird's eye chiles**

**1 garlic clove, peeled and coarsely chopped**

**1½ tablespoons Thai fish sauce**

**1 teaspoon white sugar**

**1 oz thinly sliced peeled onion,**

**1 oz carrot, peeled and cut into thin batons**

**1 scallion, finely chopped**

**2¼ tablespoons freshly squeezed lemon juice or 1½ tablespoons freshly squeezed lime juice**

**a few fresh cilantro leaves, to garnish**

*Serves 4 as part of a meal or 1 individually*

Heat the oil for deep-frying in a wok over high heat until it reaches 350°F, or until a cube of bread browns in 30 seconds. Add the chicken skin pieces and deep-fry for about 4 minutes until they are golden brown and crisp and float to the surface. Use a wire spoon or tongs to remove the chicken skin from the oil and drain well on paper towels. Set aside and leave to cool. It is important to leave the chicken skin to cool completely before it is added to the dressing, or it will become chewy and the heat from it will wilt the vegetables.

Using a pestle and mortar, grind the chiles and garlic into a paste, then transfer the paste to a bowl. Add the fish sauce and sugar and stir together.

Add the crispy chicken skin and toss together, then add the onion, carrot, scallion, and lemon juice, and toss again.

Transfer the salad a large plate and sprinkle with cilantro leaves.

Seafood salad is normally served slightly warm or at room temperature. The seafood is boiled and drained, then seasoned before the vegetables are added. As with all Thai salads, it is freshly prepared and served immediately. People who like to have a few drinks after work often order such a salad to accompany their drink (usually whisky or beer), as it is light and spicy and encourages them to sweat out the alcohol before going back home to their family. This is also a good dish after a late night out with friends for the same reason—a great recipe to prevent a hangover! The aroma and flavor of the lemongrass help to tone down any fishy smell from the seafood. Some recipes for this dish add roasted chile paste, and you can also include squid, if you like.

## Aromatic Spicy Seafood Salad with Lemongrass

Yum Ta-Lay

8–10 live mussels, cleaned and any beards removed

3¼ oz raw shrimp, peeled and deveined but with the tails left on

3 oz crab claws

2½ oz skinless fish fillet, such as monkfish, cut into chunky pieces

2 teaspoon thinly sliced lemongrass

2–3 shallots, or ½ red onion, peeled and thinly sliced

1 oz carrot, peeled and cut into thin batons

1½ tablespoons Thai fish sauce

1 teaspoon white sugar

2 fresh bird's eye chiles, pounded

1 garlic clove, peeled and crushed

1 scallion, finely chopped

2¼ tablespoons freshly squeezed lemon juice, or 1½ tablespoons freshly squeezed lime juice

a few fresh cilantro leaves, to garnish

*Serves 4 as part of a meal or 1 individually*

Bring a large pan of water to a boil over high heat. Discard any mussels with cracked shells or open ones that do not close when sharply tapped. Reduce the heat to medium, then add the mussels, shrimp, crab claws, and fish fillet, and simmer for no longer than 1–2 minutes until the mussel shells open, the shrimp and the crab claws turn pink, and the fish becomes opaque. Immediately remove the seafood from the water. Be careful not to overcook it as the texture will become very tough and chewy. Remove the shells from the mussels, discarding any whose shells have not opened.

Combine the lemongrass, shallot or red onion, and carrot in a bowl. Stir in the fish sauce, sugar, chiles, garlic, and scallion.

Add the seafood to the other ingredients, add the lemon or lime juice, and gently toss together. Transfer to a large plate and sprinkle with cilantro leaves.

# Curries

Red curry sauce really goes well with salmon. Although salmon is very common and well known in the West, it is hardly known in Thailand—I don't remember ever tasting salmon during my childhood. The inspiration for this recipe came from the fact that the color of salmon is very appealing and it is widely available. The dish is very popular among westerners as they get to use a knife and a fork which probably reminds them of eating at home! Thai curries usually come with so much sauce that they have to be put into a bowl. Any curries that can be served on a plate are considered "dry," even though they still have a sauce. Here the sauce is thicker than usual as coconut cream has been used instead of coconut milk.

# Salmon Steaks in Aromatic Dry Red Curry

Chu-Chi Pla-Salmon

grated rind of ¼ kaffir lime, pounded with 1 thinly sliced shallot to make a paste

1½ tablespoons ready-made red curry paste

2 salmon steaks or fillets, total weight about 10 oz

1 tablespoon vegetable oil

1 cup coconut cream

1½ tablespoons Thai fish sauce

1¼ teaspoons white sugar

*For the garnish*

6–8 kaffir lime leaves, 4 finely shredded, 2–4 left whole

1 fresh red chile, thinly sliced lengthwise

*Serves 4 as part of a meal or 2 individually*

Use a mortar and pestle to blend the lime and shallot paste with the red curry paste.

Half-cook the salmon steaks by boiling or steaming until they are medium-rare. Set aside and keep warm.

Meanwhile, heat the oil in a wok or large skillet over low heat. Add the mixed red curry paste and stir-fry for about 30 seconds. Pour in the coconut cream and stir constantly until the oil starts to appear on the surface. Stir in the fish sauce and sugar and continue simmering for about 1 minute or until the oil rises to the surface.

Put the half-cooked salmon steaks into the wok or skillet, cover the fish with a lid so that the heat is evenly distributed, and simmer for another 2–3 minutes, or until the fish is cooked through.

Transfer the salmon steaks to a serving plate and spoon the sauce over them. Garnish with the shredded and whole lime leaves and chile.

This clear, light and very refreshing curry should taste slightly sour, sweet, and salty, and it's delicious if you accompany it with Thai Fried Omelet (page 82). Other vegetables and fruit that are suitable to use include Chinese cabbage, green papaya, long or green beans, morning glories, and mustard greens. To save time when you make this next, double the amount of orange curry paste and freeze the leftovers until required.

# Clear Sour Orange Curry with Fish and Watermelon

Gang-Som Pla

3 cups chicken stock or water

hard white pith from ¼ small watermelon, or ½ cauliflower head, cut into ¼-inch pieces

1½ oz long beans, cut into 2-inch lengths

½ cup cooking tamarind juice (see page 16)

3 tablespoons palm sugar

3 tablespoons Thai fish sauce

1 tablespoon freshly squeezed lemon juice

*For the Orange Curry Paste*

5 shallots, peeled and chopped

½ teaspoon shrimp paste

4 dried red chiles, soaked in hot water for 15 minutes and drained

3 "fingers" fresh aromatic ginger (*kra-chai*), coarsely chopped

3½ oz boiled cod fillet

*Serves 4 as part of a meal*

To make the curry paste, use a pestle and mortar to pound the shallots, chiles, shrimp paste, and aromatic ginger together to make a paste. Add the boiled cod and continue pounding. You might find it easier to put all the ingredients in a blender and blend until a fine paste forms. If you can't find shrimp paste, leave it out, but add an extra ½ tablespoon fish sauce later on. Set aside.

Bring the stock or water to a boil in a wok over high heat. Stir in the paste, making sure it is well mixed. Lower the heat to medium, add the watermelon or cauliflower pieces, and continue simmering for about 10 minutes until they are tender. Add the beans and simmer for a couple more minutes. Season with the tamarind juice, palm sugar, fish sauce, and lemon juice. I like to use tamarind juice as well as lemon juice, and palm sugar instead of white sugar, because both have a smoother and more rounded taste. I find that lemon juice and white sugar on their own give too sharp a flavor.

Transfer to bowl and serve immediately.

Jungle Curry has always been my favorite dish. I love its spiciness without the richness of coconut milk, which makes it easy to maintain my waistline without compromising by eating tasteless food or starving myself to death. Jungle Curry is a perfect example of how herbs and spices are used to create a traditional Thai dish that is rich in flavor and aroma, but still incredibly light in texture.

You don't need to serve anything else with this, except a bowl of unflavored rice to tone down the heat of the red curry paste, although Thai Fried Omelet (page 82) also goes extremely well. Watch out, though, Jungle Curry is rather addictive...once you get started, it's quite difficult to stop eating it—it's so delicious and full of goodness! This is a superb dish for winter.

# Aromatic Chicken Jungle Curry

Gang-Pa Gai

½ teaspoon grated kaffir lime rind

3 tablespoons ready-made red curry paste

1 tablespoon vegetable oil

3 kaffir lime leaves, torn

9 oz boneless, skinless chicken meat, thinly sliced along the grain

3 cups chicken stock or water

2-inch piece fresh aromatic ginger (kra-chai), peeled and thinly sliced into batons

scant 1 cup drained, canned bamboo shoots, rinsed

1½ oz green beans, trimmed and cut into 1-inch lengths, or 1½ oz snow peas, trimmed

2 baby Thai round eggplant, or 1½ oz regular eggplant, chopped into wedges

2 teaspoons fresh dark green peppercorns

1 fresh red chile, thinly sliced lengthwise

1 fresh green chile, thinly sliced lengthwise

8 holy basil leaves, to garnish

*Serves 4 as part of a meal*

This recipe uses chicken, but you can substitute practically any main ingredient, such as fish, shellfish, meat, or other poultry. Do bear in mind, however, that shellfish needs very little cooking or it will become tough. You can tone down the heat of the curry by using less red curry paste (but you must not use green curry paste). You can also make this light curry more filling by adding chopped pumpkin at the same time as the chicken.

Begin by enhancing the ready-made red curry paste. Use a pestle and mortar to pound the grated lime rind and curry paste together. Heat the oil in a wok over low heat, then add the paste, and stir-fry for about 15 seconds. Do not let the paste burn. Add the lime leaves and stir for a further 10 seconds. This will give you the strong and aromatic red curry paste you need.

Add the sliced chicken to the wok and stir-fry, constantly tossing and turning, until it is half-cooked. Stir in the stock or water and continue cooking, stirring occasionally, until the chicken is cooked through and the juices run clear when you cut a slice.

Stir in the aromatic ginger, bamboo shoots, green beans, if using, eggplant, and peppercorns and simmer for a further 30 seconds, stirring occasionally. Stir in the snow peas, if using, half the sliced red and green chiles, and half the holy basil leaves.

Transfer the curry to a serving bowl and garnish with the rest of the chiles and basil leaves.

Massaman is one of a few curries that take time to make, as the technique involves stewing the meat, unlike any other curry. The only vegetables used are potatoes and onions. More spices are used than herbs, and roasted peanuts are added to the curry. This indicates that Massaman curry was heavily influenced by the Indian Muslims. My recipe may contain fewer spices than is traditional, because the strong aroma from different spices can sometimes overpower the actual taste of the dish. Massaman curry paste can be bought in Thai supermarkets, but if you cannot find any, use red curry paste instead. Chicken legs and thighs and beef are also often used in this curry. If you want a vegetarian version, use more potatoes and onions as other types of vegetables are not traditionally used.

# Massaman Curry with Lamb

Gang Mus-Sa-Man Kae

1 tablespoon
vegetable oil

1 tablespoon
Massaman curry paste
or red curry paste

200 g/7 oz boneless
lamb, such as leg, cut
into ¾-inch cubes

½ cup coconut cream

1 cup coconut milk

1 potato, peeled and
cut into 4 or 5 chunks

½ medium onion,
peeled and
thickly sliced

½ tablespoon roasted
peanuts

2 cardamom seeds,
roasted (if using red
curry paste)

1-inch piece
cinnamon stick,
roasted (if using red
curry paste)

1½ tablespoons
tamarind juice, or
1 tablespoon freshly
squeezed lemon juice

1½ tablespoons palm
sugar, or 1 tablespoon
white sugar

1 tablespoon
Thai fish sauce

*For the garnish*

**Fried Shallots
(page 50)**

**a few fresh
cilantro leaves**

*Serves 4 as part
of a meal*

Heat the oil in a wok over low heat. Add the curry paste and stir-fry for about 15 seconds, taking care not to let it burn.

Add the lamb cubes and stir-fry, constantly tossing and turning, for 1 minute. Stir in the coconut cream and simmer, stirring, for 4–5 minutes, then stir in the coconut milk, potato, onion, peanuts, cardamom seeds, and cinnamon stick, if using. Season with the tamarind juice or lemon juice, sugar, and fish sauce.

Leave the curry to simmer for about 20 minutes, or until the lamb cubes and the potatoes are cooked through and tender and oil starts appearing on the surface.

Transfer the curry to a bowl and garnish with the crisp shallots and cilantro leaves. This is probably the only curry which is garnished with cilantro instead of basil, another sign that its roots are in Indian Muslim food.

This is a dry and slightly sweet red curry that you can also make with beef, chicken, lamb, fish, or shellfish. Remember, however, if meat is your choice, that you must stir-fry it with the red curry paste before adding the coconut cream and simmer for slightly longer to tenderize the flesh. Vegetables that are suitable for this curry include broccoli, baby corn, green or long beans, and red or green bell peppers.

# Scallop Curry with Snow Peas

Panang Hoi-Shell

2 tablespoons vegetable oil

2½ tablespoons ready-made red curry paste

3 kaffir lime leaves, torn

⅓ teaspoon ground cumin (optional)

⅓ teaspoon ground coriander seeds (optional)

1 cup coconut cream

3½ oz shelled scallops

¼ cup coconut milk

2 teaspoons white sugar

2 teaspoon Thai fish sauce

2½ oz snow peas, trimmed

*For the garnish*

1 tablespoon coconut cream

1 fresh red chile, thinly sliced lengthwise

3 or 4 sweet basil leaves

*Serves 4 as part of a meal*

Heat the oil in a wok over low heat. Add the curry paste, lime leaves, and cumin and ground coriander seeds, if using, and stir-fry for about 15 seconds, taking care not to burn the mixture.

Gradually stir in the coconut cream, then add the scallops and the coconut milk, little by little, as needed, to thin the sauce to the consistency of gravy. Be careful not to make it too thin, however. Continue simmering until the oil begins to appear on the surface. Season with the sugar and fish sauce.

Add the snow peas and stir around for a minute or so. When the scallops are cooked through and opaque if you cut one, transfer them to a serving plate with all the liquid. Top the curry with a tablespoon of coconut cream, and garnish with the chile and sweet basil leaves. Serve immediately.

Ready-made curry paste is sold in many supermarkets, but often you end up buying more than you need. To prevent it from becoming moldy and being wasted, stir-fry all the curry paste at once with the kaffir lime leaves to add flavor. Use the amount specified in the recipe and then store the rest in a covered jar in the refrigerator, where it will keep for several months.

For a more unusual flavor try this with mixed fruit, such as apples, seedless grapes, canned lychees, and tomato chunks. The juice from the fruits makes this dish very tasty and naturally sweet. Remember to reduce the amount of sugar you add, and replace the stock with fruit juice.

# Thai Vegetable Green Curry

Gang Khew-Waaun Pauk

1 tablespoon vegetable oil

4 tablespoons ready-made green curry paste

3 kaffir lime leaves, torn

1¾ cups canned coconut milk

scant 1 cup vegetable stock or water

½ cup baby corn

2 oz broccoli, peeled and chopped into small pieces

1 oz carrot, peeled and cut into 1-inch sticks

1½ oz long or green beans, trimmed and cut into 2-inch lengths

1 cup coarsely chopped collard greens

1 cup drained canned sliced bamboo shoots

2 baby Thai round eggplant, cut into 4, or 1½ oz regular eggplant, cut into large chunks

2 oz snow peas, trimmed

3 tablespoons Thai fish sauce or 1 teaspoon salt

1 tablespoon white sugar

10 sweet basil leaves, plus a few extra to garnish

1 fresh red chile, thinly sliced lengthwise, plus a little extra to garnish

1 fresh green chile, thinly sliced lengthwise

*Serves 4 as part of a meal*

Heat the oil in a wok over low heat. Add the curry paste and kaffir lime leaves and stir-fry for about 1 minute, taking care not to burn them. Stir in the coconut milk and vegetable stock or water and continue simmering, stirring, until the oil appears on the surface.

Add the baby corn, broccoli, carrot, and beans and simmer for about 2 minutes, then add the collard greens, bamboo shoots, eggplant, and snow peas, and continue simmering for 1–2 minutes until all the vegetables are tender. Season with the fish sauce or salt and sugar, stirring well. It's a good idea to taste the curry at this point because curry paste brands vary in their saltiness. If it seems too salty, stir in more coconut milk or vegetables to absorb the salt.

Stir in the basil leaves and red and green chiles and give one good stir before transferring to a bowl. Garnish with the extra sweet basil leaves and red chile.

# In the Wok

Thai children just love this dish. You can also make it with cucumber instead of pumpkin, another of my childhood favorites. Include chicken in this recipe too, if you like, either in place of or as well as the pumpkin. Just slice it thinly, and remember to add it before the egg as it will take longer to cook.

This dish should be included as part of your main meal every day. Everyone loves it. The trick is to make sure you don't overcook the vegetables, so they are still crisp when served. You can increase the amount of sauce in the stir-fry by adding stock or water. Children love to put the sauce from this on their rice just as adults do with curry sauce. It's a good way to get your child to eat vegetables!

## Stir-fried Pumpkin with Egg

Fak-Thong Pad Kai

1½ tablespoons vegetable oil

4 large eggs

1 lb 4 oz piece pumpkin, peeled and cut into slices about 1 inch long and ¾ inch thick

4 tablespoons stock or water

2 tablespoons Thai fish sauce or ½ teaspoon salt for vegetarians

½ tablespoon white sugar

2 fresh red chiles, sliced lengthwise (optional)

*Serves 4 as part of a meal*

Heat the oil in a wok over medium heat. Break in the eggs and stir until they look like broken pieces of a well-cooked omelet, not scrambled eggs. Add the pumpkin and stock or water to keep the egg moist and toss and turn the pumpkin for about 2 minutes or until it's tender.

Season with the fish sauce or salt, sugar, and chiles, if using, and continue gently turning the pumpkin until it is tender and hot. Transfer to a serving dish.

## Stir-fried Seasonal Vegetables

Pad Pauk Roam

1½ tablespoons vegetable oil

2 garlic cloves, peeled and crushed

2¼ oz broccoli, trimmed and chopped into small pieces

2 oz carrot, peeled and sliced lengthwise

1½ oz long or green beans, trimmed and cut into 1-inch lengths

3½ oz collard greens, rinsed and chopped

2 oz snow peas, trimmed

3 tablespoons vegetable stock or water

1 tablespoon Thai fish sauce, or salt to taste for vegetarians

1½ teaspoons white sugar

*Serves 4 as part of a meal*

Heat the oil in a wok over medium heat. Add the garlic and stir around until it turns slightly brown.

Add the broccoli, carrot, and beans and stir-fry for a few seconds, then add the collard greens and snow peas, and continue stir-frying, constantly tossing and turning the ingredients, for about 30 seconds.

Stir in the stock or water, fish sauce or salt, and sugar and continue stir-frying the vegetables for about 40 seconds, by which time they should be tender, but still crisp. The dish is now ready to serve.

You can use whatever vegetables you want for this dish, but choose crisp, crunchy ones, as soft vegetables that contain a lot of water are not suitable. Once you've made your selection, cut them into similar-sized pieces and group them according to their density. This way you can stir-fry the longest-cooking ones, such as carrots and cauliflower, first, followed by those that hardly take any time at all, such as snow peas.

The main ingredients for Thai sweet-and-sour dishes are tomatoes, cucumbers, and pineapple. The other vegetables can be anything you like, as long as you include at least three main vegetables and fruit. You can also add thinly sliced chicken or pork to this dish—cook it before you start adding the vegetables. Just remember to decrease the vegetables by the same amount.

# Seasonal Vegetables with Cashew Nuts and Roasted Dry Chile

Pad Pauk Med-Ma-Moung-Him-Ma-Phaan

# Thai-style Sweet-and-Sour Seasonal Vegetables

Pad Preow-Whan Pauk

| | |
|---|---|
| 1½ tablespoons vegetable oil | Heat the oil in a wok over medium heat. Add the vegetables to the wok, starting with the thickest first, and stir-fry, constantly tossing and turning, until they are about half-cooked. Stir in the stock or water, then reduce the heat. |
| 10 oz mixed seasonal vegetables of your choice, such as baby corn, broccoli, carrots, cauliflower, long or green beans, onions, and snow peas, prepared as required | |
| 3 tablespoons vegetable stock or water | Season with the sugar, fish sauce or salt, and dark soy sauce, turn up the heat to high, and continue stir-frying for a few seconds until all the vegetables are tender but still crisp. Stir in the cashew nuts and dried chile. Transfer the vegetables to a plate and serve garnished with the cilantro leaves. |
| 2 teaspoons white sugar | |
| 1 tablespoon Thai fish sauce, or ½ teaspoon salt for vegetarians | |
| ½ teaspoon dark soy sauce | |
| ½ handful roasted cashew nuts | |
| 2 large roasted dried chiles, cut into small pieces with a pair of scissors | |
| a few fresh cilantro leaves, to garnish | |

*Serves 4 as part of a meal*

| | |
|---|---|
| 1½ tablespoons vegetable oil | Heat the oil in a wok or large skillet over medium heat. Add the carrot and baby corn and stir-fry for about 30 seconds, then add the onion, pineapple, tomato, bell peppers, cucumber, and oyster mushrooms, and stir-fry, constantly tossing and turning the ingredients. |
| 1 oz carrot, peeled and sliced lengthwise | |
| 1½ oz baby corn | |
| ¼ cup chopped onion | |
| ½ cup chopped pineapple | Stir in the stock or water, season with the fish sauce or salt, ketchup, sugar, and vinegar, and continue stir-frying and tossing all the ingredients until they are hot and just tender. Do not overcook. Tip into a serving bowl to serve. |
| 1½ oz tomato, coarsely sliced | |
| 1½ oz bell peppers, seeded and chopped | |
| 1¼ oz cucumber, cut into 4, seeded, and chopped into 1½-inch lengths | |
| 1¼ oz oyster mushrooms, trimmed | |
| 1 tablespoon vegetable stock or water | |
| 2½ tablespoons Thai fish sauce, or 1 teaspoon salt | |
| 2 tablespoons tomato ketchup | |
| 1 tablespoon white sugar | |
| 1 tablespoon white vinegar | |

*Serves 4 as part of a meal*

Lamb is not a common ingredient in Thailand. Most Thais find it smells too strong, so we tend to boil it before cooking to remove some of the smell, and combine it with other full-flavored ingredients, such as sake and fresh peppercorns as in this recipe. The sake and sesame oil are added at the last minute so their aromas can be fully appreciated. Boiling the lamb first also means it cooks quickly when it is stir-fried.

When I cook this for vegetarians, I use mushrooms, long or green beans, snow peas, and onions to replace the chicken. You can also leave out the chicken and use beef, pork, fish, or shellfish instead.

# Lamb Cubes with Sake

Gae Pad Med-Prik-Tai-Oon

8 oz boneless lamb, such as leg, cut into ½-inch cubes

1½ tablespoons vegetable oil

1 tablespoon water

1 tablespoon light soy sauce

1 teaspoon fresh dark green peppercorns

½ teaspoon white sugar

1½ oz mixed bell peppers, cored, seeded, and chopped

1½ oz carrot, peeled and cut into thin batons

1 tablespoon sake rice wine

1 teaspoon sesame oil

*Serves 4 as part of a meal*

Bring a saucepan of water to a boil over high heat. Add the lamb cubes and boil for 2–3 minutes until half-cooked, then drain well, and set aside.

Heat the oil in a wok or large skillet over medium heat. Add the lamb cubes and stir around for 1–2 minutes. Stir in the water to keep the mixture moist, followed by the soy sauce, peppercorns, and sugar.

Add the bell peppers and carrot and stir-fry, tossing and turning, until they are tender, but still crisp. Stir in the sake rice wine and sesame oil, then immediately transfer to a serving plate.

# Spicy Holy Basil Chicken and Chiles

Gai Pad Prik-Gra-Prao

1½ tablespoons vegetable oil

1 peeled garlic clove pounded with 1 fresh red chile to make a paste

7 oz boneless, skinless chicken breast portions, thinly sliced along the grain

3 oz onion, peeled and sliced

1½ tablespoons Thai fish sauce

1 teaspoon white sugar

½ teaspoon dark soy sauce

2½ tablespoons chicken stock or water

1 fresh red chile, sliced lengthwise

10 holy basil leaves

*Serves 4 as part of a meal*

Heat the oil in a wok over medium heat. Add the crushed garlic and chile and stir around for 10 seconds. Add the chicken slices and continue stir-frying, constantly tossing and turning, for 1–2 minutes until they are half-cooked.

Add the onion and stir-fry for about 10–15 seconds, then season with the fish sauce, sugar, and soy sauce, and continue stirring.

Add the stock or water, then stir in the chiles and basil leaves, and stir-fry for a further 10–15 seconds. The dish is now ready to serve.

When you are using fermented soybeans in a dish, be careful not to add too much fish sauce, as the beans are very salty. If you don't want to make this with beef, substitute pork, chicken, or shrimp. Firm monkfish cubes are also good.

You can make plenty of changes to this recipe to suit your mood. Chicken and shrimp make good substitutes for the pork, but crispy fried fish fillets cut into little pieces are commonly used too. For vegetarians, however, just use broccoli, long or green beans, snow peas, and baby corn to make this dish.

# Stir-fried Beef with Ginger and Jelly Mushrooms

Nuea Pad-Khing

1½ tablespoons vegetable oil

1 teaspoon fermented soybeans

7 oz boneless beef, thinly sliced

5 dried jelly mushrooms, soaked for 30–45 minutes, drained, and dried

2¼ oz onion, peeled and sliced

1 tablespoon Thai fish sauce

1½ tablespoons white sugar

½ tablespoon white vinegar

½ teaspoon sweet dark soy sauce

2 inches fresh ginger root, peeled and thinly sliced lengthwise

2 scallions, cut into 2-inch lengths

2 tablespoons chicken stock or water

*For the garnish*

1 fresh red chile, thinly sliced

fresh cilantro leaves

*Serves 4 as part of a meal*

Heat the oil in a wok over medium heat. Add the fermented beans and stir around for a few seconds. Do not let them burn.

Add the beef slices and stir-fry, constantly tossing and turning, for about 1 minute until the beef is half-cooked. Stir in the jelly mushrooms and onion, and season with the fish sauce, sugar, vinegar, and soy sauce.

Add the ginger and scallions and continue stir-frying for about 15 seconds, when the dish should be ready. If the dish seems too dry, stir in a little stock or water.

Transfer all the ingredients to a serving plate and garnish with red chile slices and cilantro leaves.

# Stir-fried Pork with Red Curry Paste and Long Beans

Moo Pad Prik-Khing

1½ tablespoons vegetable oil

2 tablespoons ready-made red curry paste

2 kaffir lime leaves

7 oz boneless pork, such as leg, thinly sliced against the grain

2½ tablespoons chicken stock or water

3¼ oz long or green beans, cut into 1-inch lengths

2 tablespoons sugar

1½ tablespoons Thai fish sauce, or salt to taste for vegetarians

*For the garnish*

1 kaffir lime leaf, shredded

1 fresh red chile, thinly sliced lengthwise

*Serves 4 as part of a meal*

Heat the oil in a wok over low heat. Add the red curry paste and the torn kaffir lime leaves and stir them around, taking care not to burn them.

Add the pork with the stock or water to prevent the red curry paste from burning and stir it around. Add the beans, sugar, and fish sauce or salt and continue stir-frying, constantly tossing and turning, for about 1–2 minutes until the pork is cooked through and the beans are tender-crisp.

Transfer the dish to a serving plate and garnish with the shredded kaffir lime leaf and red chile.

This is a popular dish in Thailand, but the Spicy Fish Sauce is my own version of the traditional recipe. It goes particularly well with Aromatic Chicken Jungle Curry (page 60) and Thai Fried Omelet (page 82). If you don't like squid, however, substitute shrimp, chicken, beef, or pork. Squid flesh is quite "waxy," so scoring it before cooking helps it absorb all the flavorings, and cutting it into small pieces also helps it cook faster. Nothing is worse than overcooked squid—it has a texture like an elastic band and is extremely chewy.

# Squid Sautéed with Garlic and Cilantro Roots

Pla-Muek Toaud Gra-Tiam-Prik-Tai

**14 oz cleaned squid tubes**

**2 peeled garlic cloves pounded with 2 fresh cilantro roots to make a paste**

**2 tablespoons Thai fish sauce**

**½ teaspoon white sugar**

**3 tablespoons vegetable oil**

*For the Spicy Fish Sauce (Naam Pla Prik)*

**5 tablespoons Thai fish sauce**

**3 tablespoons freshly squeezed lemon juice**

**½ teaspoon sugar**

**2 tablespoons water**

**15 fresh bird's eye chiles, finely chopped**

**6 shallots, peeled and thinly sliced**

*Serves 4 as part of a meal*

First, make the Spicy Fish Sauce by mixing together the fish sauce, lemon juice, sugar, and water. Add the chopped chiles and sliced shallots and stir together. (Thai people eat this sauce with almost everything, sprinkling it on their food in the same way Europeans add salt and pepper. You can make the sauce with crushed garlic instead of shallots, if you prefer.)

Next, cut each squid tube open to make a flat piece. Use a very sharp knife to cut a shallow criss-cross pattern on the inside of each piece of squid, then cut the squid into 2-inch pieces.

Put the garlic and cilantro paste in a bowl and stir in the fish sauce and sugar. Add the squid and use your hands to rub the flavorings in well.

Heat the oil in a wok over medium heat. Add the squid pieces and quickly stir-fry just until they curl up into a rolls. Immediately transfer to a plate before they become overcooked. Discard any excess oil, but do not discard any of the garlic and cilantro bits. They are great for mixing with rice. This is supposed to be a dry dish.

This is one of the few Thai recipes that isn't open to adaptation and variation. It should be made only with clams. To eat, you hold the clams in your hands and suck out the flesh with your teeth—it's not a very polite way of eating, and should be avoided if you're on a date!

# Stir-fried Clams with Roasted Chile Sauce

Hoi-Lai Pad Naam-Prik-Phao

| | |
|---|---|
| 14 oz live clams in their shells | Rinse the clams well and discard any with broken shells or open shells that do not close when tapped sharply. Set aside. |
| 1 tablespoon vegetable oil | |
| 2 garlic cloves, peeled and finely chopped | Heat the oil in a wok or large skillet over medium heat. Add the garlic with the roasted chile paste and stir around, adding the fish sauce and the stock or water to make the chile paste watery. |
| 1 tablespoon roasted chile paste (see page 35) | |
| 1 tablespoon Thai fish sauce | |
| 2½ tablespoons chicken stock or water | Tip in the clams and red chiles and stir constantly until the clams begin to open. Discard any clams that remain closed. |
| 3 fresh red chiles, thinly sliced lengthwise | |
| 10–15 sweet basil leaves | Add the sweet basil leaves, then transfer everything to a bowl for serving. |

*Serves 4 as part of a meal*

This dish can also be made with a whole crab, but you will have to steam the crab first, then cut it into four to six pieces, and stir-fry it as in this recipe. Alternatively, you can break eggs into the dish and fry them just before adding the crab claws.

# Stir-fried Crab Claws with Curry Powder and Celery

Gaum-Puu Pad Pong-Ga-Ree

| | |
|---|---|
| 1½ tablespoons vegetable oil | Heat the oil in a wok over medium heat. Stir in the fish sauce, curry powder, and sugar and stir to mix well. Add the crab claws and stir them around thoroughly, then stir in the water. |
| 3 teaspoons Thai fish sauce | |
| 1 teaspoon curry powder | |
| 1 teaspoon white sugar | |
| 8–10 crab claws | Continue stir-frying the crab claws, tossing and turning, until the claws are cooked and are no longer transparent. |
| 3 tablespoons water | |
| 2–3 tablespoons chopped celery | Add the celery and stir for another minute or so, then transfer the crab claws to a serving plate, and sprinkle with the pepper. |
| freshly ground black pepper, to garnish | |

*Serves 4 as part of a meal*

Monkfish is a meaty fish, but it still needs to be handled delicately. When I say "stir-fry" in the recipe, what I mean is use a spatula to lift up the ingredients and gently turn them over. That way the fish won't break into flakes. Also, don't cut the fish into too small pieces or it will fall apart during cooking.

# Monkfish with Lemongrass and Lime

Pla Pad Ta-Krai

10 oz monkfish fillet, thin membrane removed and cut into bitesize chunks (not too small)

1½ tablespoons vegetable oil

2 garlic cloves, peeled and crushed

1¼ oz lemongrass, finely chopped into rings

1 tablespoon fermented soybeans

1½ tablespoons Thai fish sauce

½ tablespoons sugar

1 tablespoon water (optional)

½ a red, orange, or green bell pepper, seeded and cut into 1½-inch slices

2 oz carrot, peeled and cut into batons

1 tablespoon freshly squeezed lime juice

a few fresh cilantro leaves, to garnish

*Serves 4 as part of a meal*

Bring a pan of water to a boil over high heat. Add the monkfish cubes and poach for about 1 minute until half-cooked. Use a slotted spoon to remove the fish from the water and set aside. Discard the cooking water.

Heat the oil in a wok over medium heat. Add the garlic and lemongrass and stir-fry for a few seconds, then stir in the fermented soybeans, followed by the monkfish cubes. Gently "stir-fry" (see above) for about 30 seconds.

Season with the fish sauce and sugar, and at this point, if the stir-fry is too dry, add the water. Add the bell pepper and carrot and stir-fry for a further 15 seconds until the monkfish is cooked through and the vegetables are tender but not overcooked. Remove from the heat and stir in the lime juice, then transfer to a serving dish, and garnish with the cilantro leaves.

This omelet should be as dry as possible otherwise the sauce will seep through, which is why no fish sauce is included in the recipe. You can make this dish with ground chicken or pork, but remember to use fewer vegetables.

# Vegetable Stuffed Omelet

Kai Yad-Sai Pauk

**2 tablespoons vegetable oil**

**a handful of mixed vegetables, such as onions, baby corns, carrots, mushrooms, garden peas, mixed bell peppers, and tomatoes, prepared as necessary and chopped**

**1½ tablespoons tomato ketchup**

**¾ teaspoon white sugar**

**¼ teaspoon salt**

**2 large eggs, beaten**

*For the garnish (optional)*

**a few fresh cilantro leaves**

**a thin piece of fresh red chile**

*Makes 1 omelet*

Heat 1 tablespoon of the oil in a skillet over medium heat. Add the chopped onion and fry until it is soft and golden, then stir in the remaining vegetables, and stir-fry for 1–2 minutes.

Season the vegetables with the tomato ketchup, sugar, and salt and continue stir-frying until they are tender but still crisp. Set aside while you make the omelet.

Wipe out the skillet, then heat the remaining oil over medium heat. Tilt the pan so the oil covers the entire surface to prevent the eggs from sticking. Once the surface is covered, discard any excess oil.

Reduce the heat to medium-low. Pour in the eggs, tilting the pan so they cover most of the surface. Leave the eggs to cook until they form a thin, set omelet, then turn off the heat.

Place the cooked vegetables in the center of the omelet. Use a metal spatula and your hand to fold each side of the omelet gently over the vegetables so the sides meet in the center.

Place a plate large enough to hold the omelet face-side down on top, then carefully invert the plate and skillet so the omelet sits nicely on the plate. Garnish with a piece of chile and cilantro leaves, if you like.

Thais love to eat omelets with Spicy Thai Fish Sauce and sliced fresh bird's eye chiles, or a particular smooth reddish-orange chile sauce called Sri Racha, which you can find at supermarkets. This is not the same as the transparent sauce that allows you to see the chile seeds, which is sweet chile and garlic sauce (labelled in Thai as *Naam Jim Gai*, which translates as "dipping for chicken").

If you like your eggs spicy, add sliced fresh chiles and scallions to the beaten eggs before frying them.

# Thai Fried Omelet

Kai Jeiw

**3 large eggs, beaten**

**1 teaspoon Thai fish sauce, or a pinch of salt for vegetarians**

**a pinch of sugar (optional)**

**2 cups vegetable oil, for deep-frying**

*To serve*

**Spicy Thai Fish Sauce (page 76)**

**smooth chile sauce**

*Serves 4 as part of a meal*

Mix the fish sauce or salt and the pinch of sugar into the eggs.

Heat the oil in a wok over medium heat—it will be hot enough when a drop of the beaten egg sizzles instantly. Pour in the beaten egg mixture and leave to fry until the underside is crisp and golden. If the oil is not hot enough, the eggs will soak up too much oil—the omelet should be crispy on the outside while the inside is cooked but still moist. You need lots of oil for this dish, so there will be plenty left over, which you can discard or reuse for deep-frying.

Flip the omelet over and continue frying until the other side is crisp and golden. The omelet is now ready to eat, but don't fold it like a Western omelet—unless you need to make it fit on the plate!

This dish is a revolutionary chicken wing recipe! Usually only Asian people order chicken wings, but this dish has changed all that. I know what my Western customers like when it comes to food, so this sauce has a slightly sweet and tangy taste, as well as being thick and spicy. The amount of sauce will only lightly coat the crispy fried chicken wings.

## Triple-flavor Chicken Wings

Peek-Gai Saam-Roaud

| | |
|---|---|
| vegetable oil, for deep-frying, plus 1 tablespoon, for stir-frying | Heat enough oil for deep-frying in a wok over high heat until it reaches 350°F, or until a cube of bread browns in 30 seconds. Add the chicken wings and deep-fry for 6 minutes, stirring them around, until golden brown. Use a wire spoon or tongs to remove the chicken wings from the oil and drain well on paper towels, then set aside. |
| 14 oz chicken wings | |
| 2 tablespoons tomato ketchup | |
| 1 tablespoon smooth chile sauce | |
| 1½ tablespoons Sweet Chile and Garlic Sauce (page 28) | Heat 1 tablespoon vegetable oil in a wok or large skillet over medium heat. Stir in the ketchup, smooth chile sauce, sweet chile and garlic sauce, and sugar and stir around. |
| ½ tablespoons white sugar | |
| 2 scallions, cut into 2-inch lengths | |
| 1½ oz carrot, peeled and cut into thin batons | Stir in the crispy fried chicken wings, making sure they are well coated with the sauce. Add the scallions and carrot and stir-fry, constantly tossing and turning, for about 1 minute, when the dish will be ready to serve. |
| *Serves 4 as part of a meal* | |

You can also use this method for chicken wings. If you want to use sliced beef, pork, or chicken, or shrimp or squid, just omit the flour and stir-fry the meat instead, using 2 tablespoons of oil.

## Deep-fried Marinated Spareribs with Garlic and Cilantro Roots

Sea-Kloung-Moo Toaud Gra-Tiam-Prik-Tai

83

| | |
|---|---|
| 2 peeled garlic cloves pounded with 2 fresh cilantro roots to make a paste | Put the garlic and cilantro paste in a bowl large enough to hold the spareribs and stir in the fish sauce and soy sauce. |
| ½ tablespoon Thai fish sauce | Add the pork spareribs to the bowl and use your hands to rub the marinade all over them. Set aside for 10 minutes. |
| ½ tablespoons light soy sauce | |
| 1 lb 4 oz pork spareribs, cut into 2-inch pieces | Heat enough oil for deep-frying in a wok over high heat to 350°F, or until a cube of bread browns in 30 seconds. Sprinkle the spareribs with the flour, then add them to the wok, and deep-fry for about 6 minutes until they are golden brown and crisp. Use a wire spoon or tongs to remove the ribs from the oil and drain well on paper towels. |
| vegetable oil for deep-frying | |
| 1 tablespoon all-purpose flour | |
| a few fresh cilantro leaves, to garnish | |
| *Serves 4 as part of a meal* | Transfer the ribs to a serving plate and sprinkle with the cilantro leaves. |

This recipe was created following the success of two other dishes, Asian Duckling (opposite) and Crispy Soft-shell Crab (page 86), and is a mixture of both. It is extremely aromatic and spicy. One of my proudest moments was when a customer ordered this dish to take away about four or five times every week for about three consecutive years. I still think of him every single time I'm cooking it!

The idea for this recipe came when I was eating a dish called "Chile Beef" at one of my favorite Chinese restaurants. On returning to the Busabong, I decided to try to make it with roast duck and Thai herbs. Finally I got it right and came up with one of the most popular dishes on our menu. Once, a regular customer rang me to complain that she had spent a fortune on Thai cookbooks, but could not find the recipe anywhere. If she's reading this, I hope it was worth the wait!

# Peppercorn Chicken with Almond Flakes

Gai-Grob Pad-Med-Prik-Tai-Oon

**1 cup all-purpose flour**

**scant ½ cup water**

**7 oz boneless, skinless chicken meat, thinly sliced**

**vegetable oil**

**1 tablespoon fermented soybeans**

**1 peeled garlic clove pounded with 1 fresh red chile to make a paste**

**2 inches fresh ginger root, peeled and thinly sliced lengthwise**

**1 tablespoon Thai fish sauce**

**1 tablespoon white sugar**

**1½ oz carrot, peeled and cut into batons**

**1 scallion, cut into 1-inch lengths**

**1 fresh red chile, sliced lengthwise**

**1 teaspoon fresh green peppercorns**

**10 holy basil leaves**

**¼ cup almond flakes**

*Serves 4 as part of a meal*

Mix ¾ cup of the flour with the water to make a smooth paste. Coat the chicken slices in the paste, lift them up, and let the excess paste drip off. Sprinkle the slices with the remaining dry flour to keep the paste on the chicken.

Heat enough oil for deep-frying in a wok over high heat until it reaches 350°F, or until a cube of bread browns in 30 seconds. Add the chicken slices and deep-fry for about 3 minutes until crisp and golden. Remove the chicken slices from the oil and drain well on paper towels. Set aside.

Heat 1½ tablespoons vegetable oil in a wok over medium heat. Add the fermented soybeans, garlic and chile paste, and ginger and stir-fry for about 30 seconds. Do not let the mixture burn. Season with the fish sauce and sugar.

Add the deep-fried chicken and toss until thoroughly coated with the sauce. Add the carrot, scallion, sliced chile, peppercorns, holy basil leaves, and most of the almond flakes and continue stir-frying and tossing for 1 minute. Garnish with the reserved almond flakes and serve immediately.

# Asian Duckling

Ped Toaud-Grob Soung-Kroung

**1 cup all-purpose flour**

**scant ½ cup water**

**5½ oz roast duck, with skin, thinly sliced**

**vegetable oil**

**2 peeled garlic cloves pounded with 2 fresh cilantro roots to make a paste**

**2 inches fresh ginger root, peeled and thinly sliced lengthwise**

**1½ tablespoons Thai fish sauce**

**1 tablespoon white sugar**

**2 oz mixed bell peppers, cored, seeded, and sliced**

**¼ cup almond flakes**

**1 scallion, cut into 1-inch lengths**

**2 roasted dried chiles, chopped**

**1 oz carrot, peeled and cut into batons**

**2 teaspoons fresh green peppercorns**

**a few fresh cilantro leaves, to garnish**

*Serves 4 as part of a meal*

Put ¾ cup of the flour in a bowl and add the water to make a smooth paste. Coat the duck slices with the flour paste, then lift them up, and let the excess paste drip off. Lightly sprinkle the slices with the remaining dry flour to hold the paste in place.

Heat enough oil for deep-frying in a wok over high heat until it reaches 350°F, or until a cube of bread browns in 30 seconds. Deep-fry the duck slices for 1–2 minutes until they are crisp and float to the surface. Remove the duck slices from the oil and drain on paper towels, then set aside.

Heat 1½ tablespoons vegetable oil in a wok over medium heat. Add the garlic and cilantro paste and ginger and stir-fry for about 15 seconds. Do not burn. Season with the fish sauce and sugar. Add a small amount of water if the sauce is too dry.

Stir in the bell peppers, almonds, scallion, chiles, carrot, and green peppercorns. Add the duck and continue stir-frying, constantly turning, until heated through. Transfer to a serving plate and garnish with cilantro leaves.

This dish has been on the Busabong menu for ten years, and is also very popular, especially among the American and Thai customers. It was also created after a visit to a Chinese restaurant, but I've adapted it to include Thai flavorings, which are much more aromatic.

To make this dish even more fragrant, you can deep-fry some extra holy basil leaves and sprinkle them on top of the soft shell crabs just before serving.

# 86 Crispy Soft-shell Crab with Chile and Holy Basil

Puu-Nim Toaud-Grob Pad Sa-Moun-Prai

1 cup all-purpose flour

1 cup water

2 prime-sized soft-shell crabs, weighing about 2½ oz each

vegetable oil, for deep-frying, plus 1½ tablespoons for stir-frying

2 peeled garlic cloves pounded with 1 fresh red chile to make a paste

1 tablespoon fermented soybeans

2 inches fresh ginger root, peeled and thinly sliced lengthwise

1 tablespoon Thai fish sauce

¾ tablespoon white sugar

2 fresh red chiles, sliced lengthwise

1 scallion, cut into 1-inch lengths

about 10 holy basil leaves

*Serves 4 as part of a meal*

Put ¾ cup of the flour into a bowl and stir in the water to make a smooth paste. Add the crabs to the bowl, coat them in the flour paste, then lift them up, and let the excess paste drip off. Lightly sprinkle both crabs with the remaining dry flour to hold the paste in place.

Heat enough oil for deep-frying in a wok over high heat until it reaches 350°F, or until a cube of bread browns in 30 seconds. Add the crabs and deep-fry for 1–2 minutes until crisp and golden. Use a wire spoon or tongs to remove the crabs from the oil and drain well on paper towels, then set aside.

Heat 1½ tablespoons vegetable oil in a wok over medium heat. Add the fermented soybeans, garlic and chile paste, and ginger and stir-fry for about 30 seconds. Do not let the mixture burn. Stir in the fish sauce and sugar. If the sauce seems too dry, stir about ½ tablespoon water into it.

Add the reserved crabs and toss thoroughly with the sauce. Add the chiles, scallion, and holy basil leaves and gently toss one more time before serving.

If you find the prospect of frying a whole fish too daunting, use fillets cut into small pieces and lightly battered (see page 86) before deep-frying. For a vegetarian version you can replace the red snapper with beancurd cubes.

# Crispy Red Snapper with Ginger and Straw Mushrooms

Pla Toaud-Jien

1 tablespoon tapioca flour

2 tablespoons water

1 red snapper, about 1 lb 10 oz, head removed, trimmed and gutted

vegetable oil, for deep-frying, plus 1½ tablespoons, for stir-frying

4 inches fresh ginger root, peeled and thinly sliced lengthwise

2 garlic cloves, peeled and crushed

1 tablespoon fermented soybeans

1½ teaspoons light soy sauce

1 teaspoon Thai fish sauce

1 tablespoon white sugar

2¼ oz dried straw mushrooms, soaked in cold water for 30–45 minutes, drained and squeezed dry

2 oz oyster mushrooms, trimmed

2 scallions, cut into 1-inch lengths

1½ cups chicken stock or water

few drops sesame oil (optional)

*For the garnish*

a few fresh cilantro leaves

freshly ground black pepper

*Serves 4 as part of a meal*

Put the tapioca flour in a small bowl and stir in the water to make a thin paste, then set aside.

Make 3 slashes, about ⅛ inch deep, on each side of the red snapper to help it cook more quickly and so the sauce can penetrate the flesh, then set aside.

Heat enough oil for deep-frying in a large wok over high heat until it reaches 350°F, or until a cube of bread browns in 30 seconds. Gently lower the fish into the oil and deep-fry for about 15 minutes, turning halfway through cooking, until it is crisp and golden brown. You can also check whether the fish is cooked by removing it from the oil and gently opening it along a slash to see if the flesh comes off the bone.

Remove the fish from the wok, drain well on paper towels, and transfer to a serving dish. Keep warm while you stir-fry the rest of the dish.

Wipe out the wok. Heat 1½ tablespoons oil in the wok over medium heat. Add the ginger, garlic, and fermented soybeans and stir-fry for about 30 seconds. Stir in the soy sauce, fish sauce, and sugar.

Add the straw mushrooms, oyster mushrooms, scallions, and chicken stock or water and stir together. Stir in the reserved tapioca flour mixture for about 30 seconds until the sauce thickens to a consistency that is slightly thinner than gravy. If you like the aroma of sesame, add a few drops of sesame oil.

Spoon the sauce and vegetables over the fish and garnish with cilantro leaves and a sprinkling of pepper.

This is a very traditional Thai dish, originally known as "Three Flavors Fried Fish." Some people like to use *Naam Jim Gai* (see page 82) as a short-cut to make this sauce, but I don't think it makes a suitable replacement. Be generous with the herbs and chiles in this recipe to make the sauce as tasty as possible. It tastes superb, and the sauce is quite runny so that it can seep into the flesh of the fish. If you don't want to fry a whole fish, you can use fish fillets, lightly battered (page 86) before deep-frying, instead.

# Holy Basil Red Snapper with Chiles and Garlic

Pla Toaud Raad-Prik

1 red snapper, about 1 lb 10 oz, head left on, but trimmed and gutted

vegetable oil, for deep-frying, plus 2 tablespoons, for stir-frying

5 peeled garlic cloves pounded with 2 fresh red chiles to make a paste

5 tablespoons white sugar

4 tablespoons Thai fish sauce

1 tablespoon white vinegar

3 tablespoons chicken stock or water

1 fresh green chile, sliced lengthwise

10 holy basil leaves

*Serves 4 as part of a meal*

Make 3 slashes, about ⅛ inch deep, on each side of the red snapper to help it cook more quickly and to allow the sauce to penetrate the flesh.

Heat enough oil for deep-frying in a large wok over high heat until it reaches 350°F, or until a cube of bread browns in 30 seconds. Gently lower the fish into the oil and deep-fry for about 15 minutes, turning halfway through cooking, until the flesh surrounding the slashes is golden, and comes away from the bone easily when the fish is opened up. Remove the fish from the wok, drain well on paper towels, and transfer to a serving plate. Keep warm while you stir-fry the rest of the dish.

Wipe out the wok and reheat it over medium heat. Add 2 tablespoons oil and the garlic and chile paste and stir for a few seconds taking care not to let it burn.

Reduce the heat and season with the sugar, fish sauce, and vinegar, followed by the stock or water, and simmer for about 30 seconds on low heat or until the sauce becomes slightly thickened. Stir in the chile and holy basil leaves, then pour the sauce over the fish.

# Out of the Wok

This dish is great to serve with Steamed Sticky Rice (page 106) and Aromatic Spicy Green Papaya Salad (page 43). If you offer the chicken with just the rice, put out some sweet chile and garlic sauce as well; you won't need the sauce if you serve it with the papaya salad.

# Broiled Spiced Chicken

Gai-Yang Busabong

**4 peeled garlic cloves pounded with 4 fresh cilantro roots to make a paste**

**1 teaspoon freshly ground black pepper**

**1 teaspoon ground cumin**

**1 teaspoon coriander seeds**

**2 teaspoons vegetable oil, plus a little extra for the broiler rack**

**2 tablespoons light soy sauce**

**2 tablespoons Thai fish sauce**

**1 tablespoon white sugar**

**1 chicken, about 3½ lb, cut in half**

*Serves 4 as part of a meal*

Put the garlic and cilantro paste in a large bowl, then stir in the black pepper, cumin, and coriander seeds. Stir in the vegetable oil and season with the soy sauce, fish sauce, and sugar. Now you have the perfect marinade. (Try it with pork, too.)

Rub the marinade all over the chicken halves, inside and out. Cover and chill for about 1 hour, then remove from the refrigerator, and leave to come to room temperature before cooking.

Meanwhile, light your barbecue and leave the coals until they are glowing, or preheat the broiler to high. Lightly grease the broiler rack. Cook the chicken on the barbecue or under the broiler for about 45 minutes, turning and basting it with any leftover marinade, until the skin is crispy and the juices run clear when you pierce a piece. Whichever method you use, it is best to cook the skin side last so it will be nice and crisp when you serve the chicken.

Alternatively, preheat the oven 350°F. Put the chicken halves in a large ovenproof dish in the middle of the oven and roast for 45 minutes–1 hour until the skin is crispy and the juices run clear when you pierce a piece.

This is a mouthwatering recipe in which juicy jumbo shrimp are dipped in a wonderful piquant sauce. Made especially for seafood, the sauce also goes wonderfully with any broiled fish or shellfish. One customer of mine ordered four portions for himself and some friends as only one of several dishes. The final bill was enormous, but he was still very happy!

# Broiled Jumbo Shrimp with Spicy Chile and Garlic Sauce

Goong Phao

vegetable oil,
for greasing

6 raw jumbo shrimp,
unpeeled and with
or without their heads,
as you like

*For the Spicy Chile
and Garlic Sauce*

4 peeled garlic cloves
pounded with 4 fresh
bird's eye chiles to
make a paste

3 tablespoons
Thai fish sauce

1½ tablespoons
freshly squeezed
lemon juice

1 teaspoon
white sugar

*Serves 2–3 as part
of a meal or
1 individually*

To make the Spicy Chile and Garlic Sauce, combine all the ingredients in a nonmetallic bowl, then set aside. This sauce is different from normal *Nam Pla Prik*, which is eaten with rice and other dishes. This is specially made to eat with plain steamed, broiled, or boiled seafood and meat, such as mussels, crab, squid, fish fillets, and pork.

Preheat the broiler to high and lightly grease the broiler rack. Use a sharp knife to butterfly the shrimp by cutting through the back from the head to the tail, without cutting all the way through.

Lay the shrimp flat on the broiler rack, flesh side down, and broil for 1–1½ minutes until the shell is slightly burnt, then turn over, and broil for a few seconds until the flesh turns pink and opaque, but is still moist. Serve the shrimp immediately with the Spicy Chile and Garlic Sauce on the side.

This dish is commonly known as "Weeping Tiger," probably because tigers are known to be very strong character animals but if you give this dish to a tiger to eat, it will cry and weep like a child because the sauce is so spicy! It would also be an appropriate dish to give to your enemy! This is definitely one of my favorite dishes. You can also use the marinade for a pork loin.

## Broiled Marinated Sirloin with Seasonings

Nuea-Yang Jim -Jaew

1 peeled garlic clove pounded with 1 fresh cilantro root to make a paste

1½ teaspoons fresh green peppercorns

1 teaspoon Thai fish sauce

1 teaspoon light soy sauce

1 teaspoon white sugar

9–10 oz steak

Steamed Sticky Rice (page 106; optional), to serve

*For the North-Eastern-Style Chile Sauce*

1 tablespoon rice

¼ cup Thai fish sauce

3 tablespoons freshly squeezed lemon juice

Bird's Eye Chile Powder, made from 10–12 bird's eye chiles, roasted, dried, and crushed

2 teaspoons white sugar

*Serves 4 as part of a meal*

Put the garlic and cilantro paste in a large bowl, then add the peppercorns, fish sauce, soy sauce, and sugar and mix together. Add the steak to the bowl and rub in the marinade so it is well coated, then let marinate for 20 minutes.

Meanwhile, to make the North-Eastern-Style Chile Sauce, toast the rice in a dry wok over low heat until golden brown all over. Immediately tip it out and grind to a fine powder using a pestle and mortar. Transfer the rice to a small bowl and add the fish sauce, lemon juice, crushed chiles, and sugar, stirring until the sugar has dissolved. Set aside.

Light your barbecue and leave the coals until they are glowing, or preheat the broiler to medium. Lightly grease the broiler rack.

When the barbecue or grill is ready, grill the steak over coals for about 3 minutes on each side for medium-rare, or under the broiler for 1½–2 minutes on each side.

Leave the steak to stand for a few minutes before slicing and serving with the North-Eastern-Style Chile Sauce and rice, if you like.

This dish has been on the Busabong menu for only a year. It was created when a good friend of mine asked for a baked or broiled fish that did not have any oil on it. She really liked it, and so we decided to put it on the menu permanently.

If you can't get hold of a sour mango for this recipe, try it with a cooking apple and finely chop half a red onion to replace the shallot.

# Baked Sea Bass with Herbs

Pla Pho Samoun-Prai

**1 sea bass, about 1 lb 10 oz, head left on, but trimmed and gutted**

**2 peeled garlic cloves pounded with 2 fresh cilantro roots to make a paste**

**1 tablespoon light soy sauce**

**1 lemongrass stalk, lightly pounded**

*For the Sour Mango Relish*

**½ small sour mango, thinly sliced or shredded**

**2 fresh bird's eye chiles, crushed**

**1 shallot, peeled and finely chopped**

**1½ tablespoons Thai fish sauce**

**1 tablespoon freshly squeezed lemon juice**

**1 teaspoon white sugar**

*Serves 4 as part of a meal or 2 individually, with rice*

Preheat the oven to 450°F. Make 3 slashes on each side of the sea bass to help the flavors penetrate.

Put the garlic and cilantro paste in a bowl and stir in the soy sauce. Rub the paste all over the fish, rubbing it well into the slashes. Put the lemongrass stalk in the fish's cavity.

Put the fish on a piece of foil large enough to enclose it, then wrap it up securely so none of the juices can escape. This will help keep the flesh moist. Put the fish on a cookie sheet and bake for 25–30 minutes until it is cooked through. Unwrap the foil and let the fish sit in the oven for another few minutes until the skin becomes slightly crisp.

Meanwhile, make the Sour Mango Relish. Place the sour mango, chiles, shallot, fish sauce, lemon juice, and sugar in a nonmetallic bowl and stir together. Set aside until it is time to serve the fish.

Transfer the fish to a large platter and serve with the Sour Mango Relish on the side.

For anyone familiar with the version that uses ginger, this dish has a quite unexpected taste. I was entertaining an English friend at the Busabong and when Sea Bass with Salted Plums was served, he assumed it was steamed with ginger as it smelled quite aromatic. He took a big bite and paused, staring at me without chewing for a few seconds and then continued chewing as normal. He later told me that he was very surprised to find out that he actually preferred it to the one with ginger sauce, as it was more refreshing and fragrant. I personally like both, depending on the mood I'm in. Salted plums can be bought from most Asian supermarkets and the spicy salted-plum mixture in this recipe can also be used with steamed mixed shellfish.

## Steamed Sea Bass with Salted Plums

Pla Noung Bouy

1 sea bass, about 1 lb 10 oz, head left on, but trimmed and gutted

1 lemongrass stalk, finely chopped

2 salted plums

2 fresh red chiles, crushed

2 garlic cloves, peeled and chopped

4 tablespoons chicken stock or water

1 tablespoon light soy sauce

1 tablespoon freshly squeezed lemon juice

½ tablespoons white sugar

3 thin lemon slices

*Serves 4 as part of a meal*

Make 3 slashes on each side of the sea bass to help it cook more quickly and so the sauce penetrates the flesh, then set aside. Heat a steamer on high so the water boils. Choose a heatproof plate large enough to hold the fish flat but that will also fit in the steamer.

Combine the lemongrass, salted plums, chiles, garlic, stock or water, soy sauce, lemon juice, and sugar, stirring until the sugar dissolves.

Pour half the spicy mixture on one side of the fish, turn the fish over and repeat on the other side. Place the sea bass on the plate and top with the lemon slices. Put the plate in the steamer, close the lid, and steam for 15–20 minutes on maximum heat, until the fish is cooked through and the flesh flakes easily if you cut into it.

You can serve these mussels with Boiled Rice (page 107), but I particularly like them on their own as a light lunch or supper with Spicy Chile and Garlic Sauce and ice-cold beer.

## Steamed Mussels with Herbs

Hoi Mang-Pu Oob Samoun-Prai

2 lb 4 oz live mussels in their shells, cleaned and any beards removed

8 kaffir lime leaves, torn

5 lemongrass stalks, lightly crushed and cut into 2-inch lengths

3 fresh cilantro roots, pounded

4 inches galangal root, thinly cut crosswise into about 10 slices

4 tablespoons stock or water

Spicy Chile and Garlic Sauce (page 93), to serve

*Serves 4 as part of a meal or 2 individually*

Heat a steamer until the water is boiling. Discard any mussels with cracked shells or that are open and do not close when sharply tapped.

Put the mussels in a shallow container that will fit inside your steamer, then add the lime leaves, lemongrass, cilantro roots, galangal root, and stock or water. Cover the steamer and steam for about 10 minutes, or until all the mussels are open. Discard any mussels that are not open. The texture of the cooked mussels should be moist, not dry. It is quite common for Thais to eat mussels when they are half-cooked, provided they are eaten with the spicy sauce in this recipe and lemon juice. The lemon juice "cooks" the mussels a little more.

Alternatively, put all the ingredients in a heavy pan over low heat, cover the pan tightly, and cook, shaking the pan back and forth, for 8–10 minutes until all the mussels open.

Serve immediately with the Spicy Chile and Garlic Sauce on the side as a dip.

Dried banana cups can be bought ready-made from most Thai supermarkets, or you can make your own using banana leaves fastened together with toothpicks to form a cup. If you can't find banana leaves, you can use any type of bowl or dish that will fit in your steamer. If you're a vegetarian, there isn't any reason to miss out on this stylish dish. Simply replace the seafood with cauliflower or broccoli, or any vegetables that are not too watery. You can also add shredded cabbage: Boil the cabbage first and squeeze out the water before placing it under the sweet basil leaves. Other options for this recipe include using chopped skinless fish fillets, such as cod, or thinly sliced chicken.

# Steamed Hidden Treasure

Hoa-Mok Talae

½ teaspoon tapioca flour

3 tablespoons coconut cream

10 sweet basil leaves

2 banana leaf cups or heatproof ramekins or bowls

1 extra large egg

2 tablespoons ready-made red curry paste, fried with oil and kaffir lime leaves (see page 60)

1½ tablespoons Thai fish sauce

½ tablespoon white sugar

9 oz prepared mixed seafood (12 oz unprepared weight), such as thinly sliced fish fillets, headless, peeled, and deveined shrimp with the tails removed, thinly sliced, cleaned squid rings, and shelled mussels

4 kaffir lime leaves, shredded

1 fresh red chile, thinly sliced lengthwise

*Serves 4 as part of a main meal*

Stir the tapioca flour into one-third of the coconut cream. Place the mixture in a small pan over low heat and heat, stirring, until it thickens, then set aside, and let cool.

Meanwhile, place half the sweet basil leaves in the base of each of the 2 banana-leaf cups or heatproof ramekins or bowls. Combine the remaining coconut cream, the egg, red curry paste, fish sauce, and sugar. Add the prepared seafood and gently stir together.

Heat a steamer on a high setting so the water is boiling. Spoon the seafood mixture into the banana cups and steam for 15–20 minutes until the mixture has set. Reduce the heat of the steamer to low, open the lid, and use a teaspoon to spoon the reserved thickened coconut cream over each banana cup, then top with the kaffir lime leaves and sliced red chile.

Close the lid on the steamer, turn up the heat again, and steam for a further 1–2 minutes to set the toppings.

Serve immediately.

This quick, simple dish, made in a similar way to steamed fish with ginger, is very popular in Thailand. I like anything cooked with ginger, but dishes taste particularly healthy when they are steamed.

You can make this dish with fish fillets, such as monkfish, or even a whole fish, in which case you should make a few slits on each side so the sauce can penetrate it, and allow a longer cooking time.

# Steamed Black Jumbo Shrimp with Ginger

Goong Noung Khing

4½ oz raw black jumbo shrimp, peeled, heads removed, and deveined

3 dried straw mushrooms, soaked in water for 15–20 minutes, squeezed dry, and thinly sliced

2 scallions, cut lengthwise into 1-inch lengths

2 inches fresh ginger root, peeled and thinly sliced lengthwise

2 tablespoons chicken stock or water

2 tablespoons light soy sauce

1 teaspoon sesame oil

1 teaspoon white sugar

*For the garnish*

1 fresh red chile, thinly sliced lengthwise

a few fresh cilantro leaves

freshly ground black pepper

*Serves 4 as part of a meal*

Heat a steamer on high until the water boils. Choose a shallow heatproof bowl large enough to hold the shrimp and that will fit in the steamer. Put the shrimp in the bowl and sprinkle with the straw mushrooms, scallions, and ginger.

Combine the stock or water, soy sauce, sesame oil, and sugar, stirring to dissolve the sugar. Pour this mixture over the shrimp.

Place the bowl in the steamer, close the lid, and steam for about 7 minutes until the shrimp are pink and curled. Take care not to over-cook the shrimp or they will be tough and chewy.

Transfer the shrimp and all the sauce to a serving bowl and garnish with the chile, cilantro leaves, and pepper.

This was another one of my favorite dishes as a child. The omelet melts in your mouth, meaning you didn't have to chew much. It has a similar texture to crème caramel, but with a savory flavor. To make a vegetarian steamed omelet, you can omit the fish flakes or salted anchovies and use salt for seasoning. But if you eat fish, you can get away without using any salt or fish sauce by increasing the amount of salted fish flakes or anchovies.

## Steamed Thai Omelet with Dried Salted Fish

Kai-Toun

2 large eggs

4 tablespoons water

½ tablespoon Thai fish sauce

½ teaspoon white sugar

1 tablespoon salted fish flakes, or chopped salted anchovies

5 shallots, thinly sliced

1 scallion, finely chopped

*For the garnish*

1 teaspoon Golden Fried Garlic (page 25)

a few fresh cilantro leaves

freshly ground white pepper

*Serves 4 as part of a meal*

Heat a steamer on high until the water boils. Beat the eggs with the water in a shallow bowl that fits inside the steamer, then stir in the fish sauce, sugar, fish flakes or chopped anchovies, shallots, and scallion.

Put the bowl of egg mixture in the steamer, close the lid, and steam for 15–20 minutes until the omelet is set and firm. Garnish with the Golden Fried Garlic and cilantro leaves and a sprinkling of white pepper.

# Rice and Noodles

This is the master recipe for many Thai rice dishes. Sticky rice is most commonly consumed in the north and northeastern regions of Thailand. It is a great favorite among children, as they don't have to use any cutlery to scoop it up as they have to do with non-sticky rice. They simply use their fingers to break the rice into bitesize portions. Eaten with Broiled Marinated Pork Skewers (page 26), I suppose it is like a Thai-style McDonald's! This recipe uses a steamer, but you will still need to start the recipe in advance as the rice must soak for several hours before cooking. Sticky rice doesn't become fluffy when cooked. I don't recommend eating it late at night as it is quite filling and will expand slightly in your stomach, leaving you feeling rather uncomfortable!

## 106 Steamed Sticky Rice for Savory Dishes

Khao-Neow Dib (uncooked rice)/Khao-Neow Noung (cooked)

**4 cups rice, soaked in cold water for 5–6 hours or overnight**

*Makes 5¾ cups cooked rice*

*Serves 4*

Sticky rice will never cook if you don't soak it in water for several hours before steaming. This is a step that you can't skip. After the rice has soaked, rinse, and drain it well.

Half-fill a steamer with water and heat it on high until the water is boiling. Remove the perforated part of the steamer and line with cheesecloth or a thin cloth. Place the rice on top and fold over the cloth to wrap.

Place the perforated part of the steamer back into position, cover, and steam for about 20 minutes over high heat until the sticky rice looks transparent and dry.

Watching rice cook is very time-consuming, so most Thais cook with an electric rice cooker nowadays. This allows you to prepare other dishes while the rice is being cooked. Electric rice cookers are very cheap and come in different sizes, shapes, and forms, so I suggest you invest in one. If you decide to cook in a pot, alternative instructions are given below.

It is best to use rice that is over 6 months old because it cooks to a lovely fluffy texture. If you can find only new rice, use a tiny bit less water, because it still contains natural moisture and the cooked texture will be too sticky and not fluffy; check the manufacturing or sell-by date on the packet before cooking.

# Boiled Jasmine Fragrant Rice or Plain Rice

Khao-Jow (uncooked rice)/Khao-Suay (cooked)

2 cups jasmine fragrant rice or plain long-grain rice

generous 2¾ cups water

*Makes 5¾ cups cooked rice*

*Serves 4*

**Using an electric rice cooker**

Put the rice in a strainer and rinse it under cold or warm running water until the water runs clear. Put the rice in the pot that comes with the electric rice cooker and add the water.

Wipe all excess water from around the outside part of the pot, then place it back in the cooker, and leave it to cook until it tells you automatically that it's ready.

Nowadays unpolished or brown rice, which is more nutritious, is quite popular because of its high vitamin and fiber content. If you prefer to use this rice, follow the instructions above but add about 4 tablespoons extra water.

**Using a pan**

Rinse the rice well as described above, then place it in a pan over medium-low heat, add the water, and bring to a boil. Make sure you keep the lid of the pan on, but stir the rice gently occasionally to avoid breaking the grains. Once the rice cooks and the water has begun to evaporate, turn the heat to very low and continue to simmer with the lid on.

Once the water has evaporated and the rice is cooked, turn off the heat, and keep the pan covered for a further 10 minutes before serving. You will not need to season the rice with salt.

This dish is slightly sweet and crunchy. Coconut cream contains a large amount of oil, so only a small quantity of vegetable oil is used to stop the rice from sticking to the wok. You should preheat the wok before the oil is added for any fried noodle or rice dish that does not have egg as one of the ingredients, to prevent the noodles or rice from sticking.

# Coconut Rice with Herbs and Spices

Khao Ga-Ti

2 teaspoons
vegetable oil

1 cup coconut cream

1 teaspoon ground
turmeric

5¾ cups cooked
Boiled Rice
(page 107)

1 tablespoon
white sugar

1 teaspoon table salt

*For the garnish*

a few pieces of
shredded carrot

a few thin pieces of
cucumber peel

a few thin fresh red
chile slices

freshly ground
black pepper

*Serves 4 as part
of a meal*

Heat a wok over medium heat, then add the oil, coconut cream, and turmeric and stir for about 30 seconds. Add the rice, sugar, and salt and continue stirring until the turmeric is well distributed throughout the rice and the rice is hot.

Tip the rice into a serving bowl and top with the shredded carrot, cucumber, chile slices, and a sprinkle of pepper.

This is a one-dish meal that Thais eat for lunch or dinner, usually accompanied with Spicy Fish Sauce (page 76). If you want something even more substantial, add your preferred choice of meat, poultry, or shrimp to the oil before you put in the chile and garlic paste, stirring until it is cooked through before you add the remaining ingredients.

# Aromatic Herbal Fried Rice with Vegetables and Crispy Fried Eggs

Khao Pad Gra-Prao Kai Doaw

4 tablespoons
vegetable oil

4 peeled garlic cloves
pounded with
2 fresh red chiles to
make a paste

5¾ cups cooked
Boiled Rice
(page 107)

4 oz onion,
peeled and sliced

4 oz collard
greens, sliced

3 oz broccoli, stalks
thinly sliced,
flowerets cut into
bitesize pieces

2 oz snow
peas, trimmed

4 teaspoons
light soy sauce

2 teaspoons
dark soy sauce

2 teaspoons
white sugar

1 teaspoon salt

a small handful
holy basil leaves

2 fresh red chiles,
sliced lengthwise

Spicy Fish Sauce
(page 76), to serve

*For the Thai
Fried Eggs*

1¾ cups vegetable oil

4 eggs

*Serves 4 as
part of a meal,
or 2 individually*

Heat a wok or skillet over medium heat, then add the oil and heat. Add the garlic and chile paste and stir around for a couple of seconds until it releases its aroma. By heating the wok first, you make sure that the oil won't be so hot that it burns the paste when you add it.

Immediately stir in the rice, followed by the onion, collard greens, broccoli, and snow peas. Stir the vegetables into the rice.

Season with the light soy sauce, dark soy sauce, sugar, and salt, stirring to distribute the brown color from the soy sauces evenly.

Add the holy basil leaves and chile slices and stir for a few seconds. Transfer to a serving dish and keep warm while you prepare the fried eggs.

To make the Thai Fried Eggs, wipe out your wok or skillet and heat the oil over medium heat. When the oil is hot, gently break in the eggs. Use a spatula or large metal spoon to lift the oil over the eggs to cook the yolks without turning the eggs over. This way the whites will be crispy, while the yolks are still runny.

Put the fried eggs on top of the rice and serve with Spicy Fish Sauce for sprinkling over them.

Chicken is a good substitute for shrimp in this popular recipe. Of course it's best to use fresh pineapple, but whole ones are quite large and you need only a small amount, so canned pineapple chunks are good enough.

For a more elaborate presentation, serve the rice in a scooped-out pineapple, rather than a bowl. Cut the pineapple in half lengthwise, scoop out the flesh to leave the center hollow, and fill with the cooked rice.

# Pineapple Fried Rice with Shrimp

Khao Pad Saub-Pa-Road

**4 tablespoons vegetable oil**

**10 raw jumbo shrimp, peeled, head and tail removed, and deveined**

**4 eggs**

**5¾ cups cooked Boiled Rice (page 107)**

**8 oz canned pineapple chunks, drained**

**¾ cup raisins**

**¾ cup fresh peas**

**½ cup diced carrot**

**2 tablespoons white sugar**

**2 teaspoons salt**

**freshly ground black pepper, to garnish**

*Serves 4 as part of a meal, or 2 individually*

Heat the oil in a wok or skillet over medium heat. Add the shrimp and stir-fry for 1 minute until they turn pink and opaque.

Break the eggs into the wok and stir constantly until they are cooked and resemble a broken omelet. Add the rice, pineapple chunks, raisins, peas, carrot, sugar, and salt and continue stir-frying for about 2 minutes until all the ingredients are well mixed.

Transfer the rice into a bowl and sprinkle with black pepper.

If you want to make this dish into a one-plate meal, fry some chicken strips or peeled and deveined shrimp after the oil is heated, but before you put in the roasted chile paste.

# Fried Rice with Roasted Chile Paste and Shredded Omelet

Khao Pad Naam-Prik-Phao

**4 tablespoons vegetable oil**

**4 tablespoons roasted chile paste (see page 35)**

**5¾ cups cooked Boiled Rice (page 107)**

**2 teaspoons white sugar**

**1¼ teaspoons salt**

*For the omelet*

**4 tablespoons vegetable oil**

**4 eggs, beaten**

*For the garnish*

**1 fresh red chile, thinly sliced lengthwise**

**a few pieces of shredded carrot (optional)**

**3–4 thin slices of lime**

*Serves 4 as part of a meal*

Heat a wok over medium heat, then add the vegetable oil. Add the roasted chile paste and stir-fry for 10 seconds. Add the rice and stir until it is well blended with the paste.

Season with the sugar and salt, stir well, then tip the rice into a serving bowl, and keep warm.

To make the omelet, heat the oil in a skillet over medium-high heat. Pour in the eggs and swirl them around the skillet to form a thin layer. Cook until the omelet is set, then tip it out of the pan. Roll up the omelet into a tight cylinder, and cut it across into thin strips.

Place the omelet strips on top of the fried rice, garnish with the chile and shredded carrot, if you like, and the slices of lime, then serve.

This can be an alternative to plain steamed rice or it can be eaten as a meal on its own. It is always best to leave the skin on roast duck when you are stir-frying it, as it helps to keep the duck moist and less oil is needed.

# Duck Fried Rice with Garlic

Khao Pad Ped Gra-Tiam

3 tablespoons vegetable oil

11 oz roasted boneless duck breast, with the skin on, chopped into small pieces

6 dried straw mushrooms, soaked in water for 1 hour, drained, and squeezed dry

4 garlic cloves, peeled and crushed

4 eggs

5¾ cups cooked Boiled Rice (page 107)

3 tablespoons light soy sauce

3 teaspoons white sugar

1¾ teaspoons salt

*For the garnish*

1 scallion, finely chopped

a few fresh cilantro leaves

*To serve*

lemon wedges

Spicy Fish Sauce (page 76)

cucumber slices

*Serves 4 as part of a meal*

Heat the oil in a wok over medium heat. Add the duck, mushrooms, and garlic and stir-fry, constantly tossing and turning them, for about 30 seconds.

Break the eggs into the wok and stir constantly until they are cooked and resemble a broken omelet. Add the rice, season with the soy sauce, sugar, and salt, and continue stir-frying and tossing until all the ingredients are well mixed.

Tip the rice into a serving bowl and garnish with the scallion and cilantro leaves. Serve with lemon wedges for squeezing over, Spicy Fish Sauce, and cucumber slices on the side.

Fried rice dishes with eggs are very easy to make, as egg prevents the rice from sticking to the wok or pan. This recipes includes chicken slices, but you can just as easily use peeled and deveined shrimp or sliced meat.

# Egg Fried Rice with Chicken

Khao Pad Gai

4 tablespoons
vegetable oil

1 lb 2 oz boneless,
skinless chicken, thinly
sliced along the grain

4 eggs

5¾ cups cooked
Boiled Rice
(page 107)

2 tablespoons
light soy sauce

2½ teaspoons
white sugar

2 teaspoons salt

3 oz onion, peeled
and sliced

2 large tomatoes,
cut into 4

*For the garnish*

a few fresh
cilantro leaves

a pinch of ground
white pepper

*To serve*

lemon wedges

Spicy Fish Sauce
(page 76)

halved cucumber slices

*Serves 4 as part
of a meal*

Heat the oil in a wok over medium heat. Add the chicken slices and stir-fry for 1–2 minutes until all the slices are cooked through and the juices run clear if you cut one piece.

Break the eggs into the wok and stir constantly until they are cooked and resemble a broken omelet. Add the rice, season with the soy sauce, sugar, and salt, and continue stir-frying until all the ingredients are well mixed.

Add the onion and tomato and continue stir-frying for 30 seconds to heat through and distribute them through the rice.

Tip the rice into a bowl, garnish with the cilantro leaves and a sprinkling of white pepper, and serve with lemon wedges for squeezing over, Spicy Fish Sauce, and cucumber slices on the side.

*Tom-Yum* is the name for noodle dishes that are made with wide rice noodles, rather than egg noodles. This soup is different from ordinary soups because it contains crushed peanuts and a wonderful blend of spicy, sour, and sweet flavors.

## Rice Noodle Soup with Ground Pork, Tom-Yum Style

Guay-Tiew Sen-Yai Tom-Yum Moo-Saub

5½ oz dried wide rice noodles, soaked in cold water for 2 hours and drained well

2 cups fresh bean sprouts

3¾ cups chicken or vegetable stock or water

2 garlic cloves, peeled and lightly pounded

2 fresh cilantro roots, lightly pounded

1¾ cups ground pork

4 tablespoons Thai fish sauce

4 tablespoons white sugar

3 tablespoons white vinegar

4 tablespoons crushed salted peanuts

2 teaspoon dried/salted cabbage (see page 118)

1 teaspoon Bird's Eye Chile Powder (page 95)

3 tablespoons freshly squeezed lemon juice

*For the Chiles in Vinegar*

5 fresh red or green chiles, chopped into fine rounds

generous ¼ cup white vinegar

*For the garnish*

a few fresh cilantro leaves

freshly ground black pepper

2 teaspoon Golden Fried Garlic (page 25)

*To serve*

Bird's Eye Chile Powder (page 95)

Thai fish sauce

white sugar

*Serves 4 as part of a meal or 2 individually*

First, make the Chiles in Vinegar by leaving the chopped chiles to soak in the vinegar for a couple of hours.

Fill a wok or pan with water and bring it to a boil over high heat. Add the noodles and bean sprouts and continue boiling for about 1 minute until the noodles are soft and the sprouts are half-cooked. Drain well, transfer the noodles and sprouts to a serving bowl, and set aside.

Bring the stock or water to a boil in the same wok or pan and add the pounded garlic and cilantro roots. Reduce the heat and simmer for about 2 minutes until the garlic and cilantro roots release their aroma.

Separate the strands of ground pork and add them to the simmering liquid. Carefully skim all the gray foam from the surface while the pork cooks, so the soup remains clear. Season with the fish sauce, sugar, and vinegar.

When the pork is cooked and no longer pink, add the peanuts, salted cabbage, and Bird's Eye Chile Powder and continue simmering for a few seconds.

Pour the soup over the noodles and bean sprouts in the bowl, then add the lemon juice. Garnish with the cilantro leaves, black pepper, and Golden Fried Garlic. Serve with the Chiles in Vinegar, Bird's Eye Chile Powder, fish sauce, and sugar for each diner to season their own soup as they wish.

I would never have thought to make a vegetarian noodle soup—not only is it unheard of in Thailand, but none of my customers has ever requested it. The credit for this recipe has to go to my son, Timothy, who forced me to make it for him. It's on the menu simply because

Timothy was eating it when another customer said "I'll have what he's having!" You will find dried salted cabbage (*Tang-Chai*) in Thai or Chinese supermarkets, but if it is unavailable, just leave it out. You can also use thin instead of wide noodles, if you prefer.

# Rice Noodle Soup with Bean Sprouts and Broccoli

Guay-Tiew Sen-Yai Naam Jae

4½ oz broccoli, trimmed and chopped into small flowerets

2 cups bean sprouts

5½ oz dried wide rice noodles, soaked in cold water for 2 hours and drained well

3¾ cups vegetable stock or water

4 garlic cloves, peeled and lightly pounded

4 fresh cilantro roots, lightly pounded

3 tablespoons Thai fish sauce, or ½ teaspoon salt for vegetarians

1 tablespoon white sugar

2 teaspoons dried salted cabbage (*Tang-Chai*)

*For the garnish*

2 teaspoon Golden Fried Garlic (page 25)

2 scallions, chopped

a few fresh cilantro leaves

freshly ground black pepper

*To serve*

Chiles in Vinegar (page 117)

Bird's Eye Chile Powder (page 95)

Thai fish sauce

white sugar

*Serves 4 as part of a meal or 2 individually*

Bring a pan of water to a boil. Add the broccoli and boil for 15 seconds, then add the bean sprouts and noodles, and continue boiling for a further 15 seconds, or until the noodles are soft. Drain the noodles and vegetables, transfer them to a large bowl, set aside, and keep warm.

Bring the water or stock to a boil in a wok or pan over high heat. Add the garlic and cilantro roots. Reduce the heat and simmer for about 2 minutes so that the cilantro roots and garlic release their aromas. Season with fish sauce, sugar, and salted cabbage and continue simmering for a few seconds.

Pour the soup over the vegetables and noodles and serve, garnished with the Golden Fried Garlic, scallions, cilantro leaves, and a sprinkling of pepper. Serve with the Chiles in Vinegar, Bird's Eye Chile Powder, fish sauce, and sugar for each diner to season their own soup as they wish.

There are many variations of this recipe to suit a range of occasions. For vegetarians, omit the chicken, increase the amount of vegetables, and season with light soy sauce rather than fish sauce.

If you don't have light soy sauce, just add a bit more Thai fish sauce or salt. Sliced pork and shrimp can be used instead of chicken, and you can always add fresh bean sprouts with the other vegetables.

## Stir-fried Wide Rice Noodles with Chicken and Vegetables

Guay-Tiew Sen-Yai Pad See-Ew Gai

1½ tablespoons vegetable oil

4½ oz boneless, skinless chicken, thinly sliced

1 egg

3½ oz dried wide rice noodles, soaked in cold water for 2 hours and drained well

3½ oz broccoli, trimmed and cut into small pieces

2½ oz collard greens or Savoy cabbage, coarsely chopped

1 tablespoon Thai fish sauce

1 tablespoon white sugar

1½ teaspoons dark soy sauce

½ tablespoon light soy sauce

2 tablespoons chicken stock or water (if needed)

freshly ground black pepper

*To serve*

**Chiles in Vinegar (page 117)**

**Bird's Eye Chile Powder (page 95)**

**Thai fish sauce**

**white sugar**

*Serves 4 as part of a meal or 2 individually*

Heat the oil in a wok over medium heat. Add the chicken slices and stir-fry, constantly tossing and turning, for about 2 minutes until the chicken is cooked through and the juices run clear when you slice a piece. Break in the egg and stir with the chicken until cooked. This should take about 1 minute.

Add the noodles to the wok and stir them around, then stir in the broccoli and collard greens or Savoy cabbage. Season with the fish sauce, sugar, and soy sauces, stirring constantly. If the mixture looks too dry, stir in just enough stock or water to keep the noodles moist.

Transfer to a serving dish and sprinkle with black pepper. Serve with the Chiles in Vinegar, Bird's Eye Chile Powder, fish sauce, and sugar for each diner to season their own plate as they wish.

The literal translation of this dish's title is "Noodles for the Drunks!" As I have mentioned in other recipes, the Thais like to accompany drinks such as beer and whisky with spicy dishes to sweat out the alcohol, and this is another of those dishes. It keeps them awake and lively as it is very spicy and quite herbal. It is also great for lunch on its own, just as you would have a plate of pasta. Beef, chicken, shrimp, or pork can be added to this dish if you reduce the amount of vegetables.

# Stir-fried Aromatic Spicy Noodles with Vegetables and Holy Basil

Guay-Tiew Sen-Yai Pad Kee-Moaw Jae

2 tablespoons
vegetable oil

2 peeled garlic cloves
pounded with ½ fresh
red chile to a paste

3½ oz dried wide rice
noodles, soaked in
cold water for 2 hours
and drained well

2½ oz broccoli,
trimmed and chopped

2¼ oz collard greens
or Savoy cabbage,
coarsely chopped

1 oz snow peas,
trimmed

1 oz long or green
beans, cut into
1-inch lengths

1 tablespoon
Thai fish sauce or ½
teaspoon salt for
vegetarians

½ tablespoon
white sugar

½ tablespoon
light soy sauce

2 teaspoons
dark soy sauce

½ fresh red chile,
sliced lengthwise

10 holy basil leaves

*Serves 4 as
part of a meal or
2 individually*

Heat a wok or large skillet over high heat. Once the wok is hot, turn the heat to medium and add the vegetable oil, followed by the garlic and chile paste and noodles. Stir-fry, constantly tossing and turning, for about 1 minute, until the noodles are soft.

Immediately add the broccoli, collard greens or cabbage, snow peas, and beans and continue stir-frying. Season with the fish sauce, sugar, and soy sauces, stirring constantly to distribute the brown color from the sauces evenly through the noodles. If the noodles seem too dry, stir in a little water.

Add the chile and basil leaves and stir them through the noodles. Tip the noodles onto a plate and serve.

This dish is probably a Thai version of pasta that uses gravy instead of a tomato sauce. It is quite filling, and very popular—I don't think I've ever met a Thai person who doesn't like it! In Thailand it is also often made with vermicelli noodles, and Chinese broccoli is used instead of the collard greens and broccoli.

# Stir-fried Rice Noodles Topped with Pork in Gravy

Guay-Tiew Sen-Yai Laad-Na Moo

1½ tablespoons tapioca flour

½ cup water

3 tablespoons vegetable oil

3½ oz dried wide rice noodles, soaked in cold water for 2 hours and drained well

2 garlic cloves, peeled and crushed

3½ oz boneless pork, such as leg, thinly sliced against the grain

1 tablespoon fermented soybeans

1½ cups chicken stock or water

2 oz collard greens or Savoy cabbage, coarsely chopped

1¼ oz broccoli, trimmed and cut into small pieces

1 oz snow peas, trimmed

1 tablespoon Thai fish sauce

½ tablespoon sugar

1 teaspoon light soy sauce

½ teaspoon dark soy sauce

freshly ground black pepper, to garnish

*To serve*

Chiles in Vinegar (page 117)

Bird's Eye Chile Powder (page 95)

Thai fish sauce

white sugar

*Serves 4 as part of a meal or 2 individually*

Put the tapioca flour in a small bowl and gradually stir in the water to make a thin, smooth paste, then set aside.

Heat a wok or large skillet over high heat. Add 1½ tablespoons of the oil, turn the heat to medium, add the noodles, and stir-fry, constantly tossing and turning, for about 1 minute until the noodles are soft. If they are too dry, add 1 tablespoon water and stir until the liquid is absorbed into the noodles. Tip the noodles onto a plate and keep warm.

To make the gravy, heat the remaining oil in the wok or skillet. Add the garlic and pork slices and stir-fry, constantly tossing and turning, for 1–2 minutes until the pork slices are almost cooked through.

Stir in the soybeans and continue stirring for a further few seconds. Add the stock or water and bring to a boil, then stir in the collard greens or cabbage, broccoli, and snow peas. Season with the fish sauce, sugar, and soy sauces and continue to stir until the vegetables are tender but still crisp.

Add the dissolved tapioca flour and stir until the sauce thickens to the consistency of gravy. Pour the pork and vegetables, with all the gravy, over the noodles and sprinkle with black pepper. Serve with the Chiles in Vinegar, Bird's Eye Chile Powder, fish sauce, and sugar for each diner to season their own noodles as they wish.

Pad-Thai is the most famous noodle dish in Thailand and is mainly available in and around Bangkok. When you order it as a take-out, it is wrapped in a cut banana leaf with a sheet of old newspaper as an outside wrapper, then sealed with a tiny wooden pin. This is my version of the classic. Some recipes include dried shrimp mixed with tiny fresh shrimp, but I find them quite chewy, so I leave them out. I also omit beancurd cake, another traditional ingredient, as I find the smoky smell too strong. Chives are authentic, but I think scallions make a great substitute. Pickled turnips (*Hoa Chai-Pho*) can be bought in Asian supermarkets.

## 122 Pad-Thai
Pad-Thai Goong

2 tablespoons
vegetable oil

5 raw black jumbo
shrimp, peeled, heads
removed, and
deveined

1 oz cooked shrimp

1 egg

3½ oz dried rice
noodles, soaked in
cold water for
about 2 hours, and
drained well

1½ tablespoons
Thai fish sauce

1½ tablespoons
white vinegar

chicken or vegetable
stock or water
(optional)

1 tablespoon chives,
cut into 1-inch pieces

1 tablespoon
peeled grated carrot

1½ cups bean sprouts

1½ tablespoons
crushed salted
peanuts

1 tablespoon crushed
pickled turnips
(*Hoa Chai-Pho*)

1 tablespoon
white sugar

*For the garnish*

**a few fresh
cilantro leaves**

**crushed dried chiles
(optional)**

*To serve*

**Chiles in Vinegar
(page 117)**

**lemon or lime wedges**

*Serves 4 as
part of a meal or
2 individually*

Heat a wok over high heat. Add the oil, turn the heat to medium, add the raw shrimp, and stir-fry for about 30 seconds until they are half-cooked. Add the cooked shrimp and crack in the egg and keep stirring until the egg looks like uneven, broken pieces of a well-cooked omelet. This should take around 45 seconds.

Immediately stir in the noodles, season with fish sauce and vinegar, and continue stir-frying, constantly tossing and turning the ingredients, but taking care not to break the noodles. Brands of noodles vary and you must be observant at this stage. If the noodles look too dry, stir in a little stock or water to help soften them. (If you have used fresh noodles, however, a little vegetable oil would be a better choice as they tend to stick to the wok when water or stock is added.)

Stir in the chives, then add most of the carrot, most of the bean sprouts, some of the peanuts, the turnips, and sugar, stirring until all the ingredients are blended.

Tip the noodles onto a serving plate and garnish with the reserved carrot, bean sprouts, and peanuts, along with the cilantro leaves and dried chiles, if you like. Serve with Chiles in Vinegar and lemon or lime wedges on the side.

This is an old recipe that is rarely cooked nowadays in Thailand, and is not at all a well-known dish among westerners either. My grandmother used to make it for me after school, and ever since she passed on, it has never been quite the same for me. It tastes very similar to Pad-Thai, and even the ingredients are quite similar, but the main differences are that this dish uses coconut milk and has fermented soybeans as a base, whereas Pad-Thai uses crushed peanuts and no coconut milk. If you don't have any tamarind juice, use a slightly smaller quantity of lemon juice. Ground pork can also be substituted for the shrimp. Banana buds can be found in Thai supermarkets—they look like a larger version of a closed lotus, and are a similar purple-pink color.

# Fried Rice Vermicelli with Coconut Milk

Mee Ga-Ti

1½ cups coconut milk

3 oz chives or scallions, cut into 1-inch lengths

2 shallots, peeled and thinly sliced into rings

5½ oz raw shrimp, peeled, heads and tails removed, and chopped

1½ tablespoons fermented soybeans

1½ tablespoons tamarind juice (see page 16)

1½ teaspoons sugar

½ teaspoon Bird's Eye Chile Powder (page 95)

2 tablespoons diced firm smoked beancurd (optional)

4½ oz dried rice vermicelli, soaked in cold water for 2 hours and drained well

*For the garnish*

1-egg Thai Fried Omelet (page 82), rolled in a thin cylinder and cut to make thin strips

1 fresh red chile, sliced lengthwise

a few fresh cilantro leaves

*To serve*

2½ cups fresh bean sprouts

lime or lemon wedges

fresh chives (optional)

sliced scallions (optional)

banana buds (optional)

*Serves 4 as part of a meal or 2 individually*

Cook the coconut milk, chives or scallions, and shallots in a wok or pan over a medium heat. Add the shrimp and continue simmering, stirring occasionally, for about 2 minutes until they turn pink and opaque. Season with the fermented soybeans, tamarind juice, sugar, and Bird's Eye Chile Powder, adding the beancurd, if using.

Remove half the sauce from the pan and set aside. Add the noodles to the sauce remaining in the pan and stir-fry for about 3 minutes until they are well mixed in and cooked. Tip the noodles onto a serving plate, then top with the remaining sauce.

Garnish the noodles with the shredded omelet, red chile, and cilantro leaves. Serve with the bean sprouts and lime or lemon wedges on the side of the plate. Serve with extra chives, scallions, and banana buds, if using.

The sauce for these noodles usually includes shallots and garlic, but I prefer it without. If you keep the flavors simple, children will enjoy this dish as well. If you want a vegetarian version, just omit the shrimp. This dish is also commonly made with pork, or a combination of pork and shrimp.

Pickled garlic (*Gra-Tiam Doung*) is a Thai delicacy that can be bought in Asian supermarkets. If you can't find any, don't replace it with ordinary garlic—leave it out.

# Crispy Caramelized Noodles with Shrimp

Mee-Grob

3 cups vegetable oil, for deep-frying, plus 1½ tablespoons, for stir-frying

3½ oz dried rice vermicelli

1 egg white, beaten

4 raw shrimp, peeled, heads and tails removed, and chopped

8 tablespoons tomato ketchup

3½ tablespoons palm sugar or 2½ tablespoons white sugar

1 tablespoon white vinegar

½ teaspoon salt

*For the garnish*

3 pickled garlic cloves (*Gra-Tiam Doung*), thinly sliced (optional)

1 fresh red chile, sliced lengthwise

a few fresh cilantro leaves

*To serve*

¾ cup fresh bean sprouts

1 or 2 chives or scallions, cut into 1-inch lengths

*Serves 4 as part of a meal or 2 individually*

Heat the vegetable oil in a wok or deep-fat fryer until it reaches 410°F. To check whether the oil is hot enough, add a small amount of rice vermicelli—it should expand and become crisp immediately. Add the rest of the rice vermicelli and deep-fry for about 10 seconds until crisp. Use tongs or a wire spoon to remove the noodles from the oil and drain on paper towels.

Next, lower the heat to 350°F, slowly drizzle the beaten egg white into the oil, and deep-fry for about 15 seconds until it becomes crisp. Remove it from the oil and drain well. Finally add the shrimp and deep-fry until they turn pink and curl. Remove them from the oil and drain well.

To make the sauce, heat 1½ tablespoons vegetable oil in a wok over medium heat. Stir in the ketchup, sugar, vinegar, and salt and simmer for 3–4 minutes, or until thickened, stirring constantly. As soon as the sauce thickens, stir in the fried shrimp.

Turn off the heat, add the crisp noodles to the wok and gently stir until the noodles are lightly coated in the sauce and stick together. Transfer to a serving plate and top with the fried egg white. Garnish with the pickled garlic cloves, if you like, and the chile and cilantro leaves. Serve with the bean sprouts and chives or scallions on the side.

This is great quick dish for a light lunch and is very popular among Thai people. It is also very healthy as the only oil used comes from the Golden Fried Garlic. You can make this dish with pork (in which case you can garnish the dish with crushed, salted peanuts), or beef, but then you will need to add an extra teaspoon of dark soy sauce rather than peanuts.

# Boiled Rice Noodles with Chicken

Guay-Tiew Sen-Lek Haang Gai

12 oz boneless, skinless chicken, thinly sliced

3 oz dried thin rice noodles, soaked in cold water for 2 hours and drained well

1 cup fresh bean sprouts

1 teaspoon Golden Fried Garlic (page 25)

1½ tablespoons Thai fish sauce

½ tablespoon white sugar

1 tablespoon light soy sauce

1 teaspoon dark soy sauce

*For the garnish*

1 teaspoon dried salted cabbage (see page 118)

½ teaspoon Bird's Eye Chile Powder (page 95)

1 scallion, chopped

a few fresh cilantro leaves

freshly ground black pepper

*To serve*

lemon wedges, for squeezing

Chiles in Vinegar (page 117)

Bird's Eye Chile Powder (page 95)

Thai fish sauce

white sugar

*Serves 4 as part of a meal or 2 individually*

Bring a large pan of water to a boil over high heat. Add the chicken slices and boil for about 2 minutes until they are cooked through and the juices run clear if you cut a slice.

Add the noodles and bean sprouts and continue boiling for another minute, or until the noodles are soft. Drain well and transfer the chicken, noodles, and bean sprouts to a serving bowl.

Add the Golden Fried Garlic, fish sauce, sugar, and soy sauces to the noodles and mix them in well, using a fork. Make sure the brown color is evenly distributed.

Top the noodles with the dried salted cabbage, Bird's Eye Chile Powder, scallion, cilantro leaves, and a sprinkling of pepper. Squeeze fresh lemon juice over to taste. Serve with the Chiles in Vinegar, Bird's Eye Chile Powder, fish sauce, and sugar for each diner to season their own noodles as they wish.

Frozen crab meat is easier to find than fresh (and certainly less expensive), but it does need to be quickly blanched first. If you can find the chunky freshly cooked crab meat, however, skip the blanching and add it straight to the noodles. If you can't find fresh noodles, use instant or dried ones, but let them cook a little longer. Dried egg noodles are always a good idea when you are short of time, as they don't require lengthy soaking.

# Boiled Egg Noodles with Crab Meat

Ba-Mee Haang Puu

5½ oz fresh
egg noodles

1 cup fresh
bean sprouts

2 tablespoons
Thai fish sauce

1 teaspoon Golden
Fried Garlic (page 25)

1 tablespoon
white sugar

2 oz shelled
crab meat, thawed
if frozen

*For the garnish*

1 scallion,
finely chopped

1 teaspoon dried
salted cabbage
(see page 118)

½ teaspoon Bird's
Eye Chile Powder
(see page 95)

a few fresh
cilantro leaves

freshly ground
black pepper

*To serve*

lemon wedges,
for squeezing

Chiles in Vinegar
(page 117)

Bird's Eye Chile
Powder (page 95)

Thai fish sauce

white sugar

*Serves 4 as
part of a meal or
2 individually*

Bring a large pan of water to a boil over high heat. Add the egg noodles and boil for about 1 minute, until they are soft. Add the bean sprouts and continue boiling for a further 10 seconds. Drain well and transfer the noodles and bean sprouts to a serving bowl.

Add the fish sauce, Golden Fried Garlic, and sugar to the noodles and mix them in well, using a fork.

Bring some fresh water to a boil and blanch the crab meat for a few seconds. Drain it well and sprinkle it over the top of the noodles. Garnish the noodles with the scallion, salted cabbage, Bird's Eye Chile Powder, cilantro leaves, and a sprinkling of black pepper.

Squeeze over fresh lemon juice to taste and serve with the Chiles in Vinegar, Bird's Eye Chile Powder, fish sauce, and sugar for each diner to season their own noodles as they wish.

# Drinks and Desserts

The strength of the coffee depends solely on your preference, but remember it will be mixed with ice, so it should have a good strong taste to begin with. Serve these tall drinks with straws so you don't get a mouthful of crushed ice.

If you don't have evaporated milk to make the white iced coffee, you can use whole milk, but the flavor will be weaker.

# Thai Iced Coffee

O-Leang (black), Ga Fae Yen (white)

**3 cups water**

**3 tablespoons freshly ground strong coffee**

**6 tablespoons white sugar**

**enough crushed ice to fill 4 highball glasses, to serve**

*For White Thai Iced Coffee*

**½ cup evaporated milk**

*Serves 4*

To make Black Thai Iced Coffee, bring the water to a boil in a pan over medium heat. Stir in the ground coffee, then add the sugar, stirring until everything dissolves. Leave to simmer over low heat for 10–15 minutes, then remove from the heat, and let cool.

To serve, fill 4 highball glasses with crushed ice, pour in the coffee, and stir to chill.

If you want White Thai Iced Coffee, stir 2 tablespoons evaporated milk into each glass.

You can add a slice of lime or lemon to the tea, if you wish. The tea has to be strong as it will be mixed with ice and sugar, but this really depends on your preference. Thais prefer their iced tea quite sweet.

# Thai Iced Tea

Cha Duam Yen (black), Cha Yen (white)

**3 cups water**

**2 tablespoons tea leaves (preferably the Thai brand specially for iced tea)**

**6 tablespoons white sugar**

**enough crushed ice to fill 4 highball glasses**

*For White Thai Iced Tea*

**½ cup evaporated milk**

*Serves 4*

To make Black Thai Iced Tea, bring the water to a boil in a pan over medium heat. Stir in the tea leaves, turn off the heat, and leave the tea leaves to steep for 10–15 minutes, depending on how strong you like your tea.

Strain out the tea leaves, then stir in the sugar, stirring until it dissolves. Leave the tea to cool.

To serve, fill 4 highball glasses with crushed ice, pour in the tea, and stir to combine.

If you want White Thai Iced Tea, stir 2 tablespoons evaporated milk into each glass.

Do not chop or slice the lemongrass for this drink. Instead, just lightly pound the stalks so they release their aroma quickly in the hot water. Keeping the stalks in single pieces also makes them easier to remove from the pot, without having to strain or filter them out. The cold version is wonderfully refreshing after a sauna or a steam-room session.

## Lemongrass Drink

Naam Ta-Krai Yen (chilled), Naam Ta-Krai Roaun (hot)

3 cups water

4 lemongrass stalks, lightly crushed

3 tablespoons white sugar or honey

ice cubes, to serve (optional)

Serves 4

Bring the water to a boil in a small pan over medium heat. Add the lemongrass stalks, reduce the heat, and simmer for about 7 minutes, or until the color begins to turn yellow.

Remove the lemongrass stalks and stir in the sugar or honey, stirring until dissolved, and set aside to cool completely.

Once the drink is cool, put the ice cubes in 4 tall highball glasses and pour it over them. Use a long spoon to stir and chill. If, however, you prefer the drink without ice, reduce the amount of sugar or honey and chill in the refrigerator.

To make a hot lemon grass drink, simmer the drink for 10 minutes, then serve in individual cups with a bowl of sugar or a small pitcher of honey on the side. For a shortcut, follow the instructions for a quick microwaved version of the Ginger Drink on page 134, replacing the ginger with lemongrass.

This recipe is so versatile it can also be made as a hot snack with sweet potatoes. Peel and dice 2 sweet potatoes (about 2 oz), add them to the boiling liquid with the ginger root, and simmer for 10–15 minutes until they are tender. Sweeten to taste, then ladle the sweet potatoes and ginger-flavored liquid into a bowl. Have this during the winter months. It is very soothing and keeps you warm.

Try making this drink with lychees, mangoes, melons, raspberries, or strawberries, rather than watermelon. Alternatively, try a mixture of fresh fruit and fruit juice, such as strawberries and orange juice; mangoes go well with mango juice and a splash of lemon juice to make the drink more refreshing. Experiment and you'll soon know which flavor combinations work for you.

## Ginger Drink

Naam Khing Yen (chilled), Naam Khing Rouan (hot)

## Frozen Watermelon Drink

Naam Tang-Mo Phan

**3 cups water**

**4 oz ginger root, peeled, cut into 3 or 4 pieces and pounded**

**3 tablespoons white sugar or honey**

**ice cubes, to serve (optional)**

*Serves 4*

Bring the water to a boil in a pan over high heat. Add the ginger, reduce the heat to medium, and continue to boil for about 10 minutes.

Remove the ginger pieces and stir in the sugar or honey. If you want a hot drink, it is now ready to serve, otherwise set aside and let cool.

Put the ice cubes in 4 glasses and pour over the cool drink. Serve with long spoons to stir the ice to make the drink even colder. If you would rather omit the ice, reduce the amount of sugar or honey and leave the drink to chill in the refrigerator.

A shortcut for making the hot drink is to pound one-quarter of the ginger and put it in a microwave-safe individual teapot. Add boiled water to halfway up the pot and microwave on high for 1½ minutes until the ginger releases its aroma. Stir a small amount of brown sugar into the pot and the drink will have the same yellowish color as if you had made it the proper way.

**1 lb fresh watermelon, peeled and cut into small pieces**

**1½ cups water**

**¾ cup sugar syrup**

**2 cups ice cubes**

*Serves 4*

Put all the ingredients in a blender and process until the ice cubes and fruit are blended to a thick and smooth texture.

I always think it is best to add the rich coconut cream to individual portions, as not everyone likes this with coconut cream. Other suitable additions include strips of fresh coconut flesh and jackfruit slices. Canned jackfruit works just as well. The coconut milk in the title of the recipe comes when the coconut cream topping is mixed with the syrup.

## Chilled Ruby Water Chestnuts in Syrup and Coconut Milk

Tub-Tim Grob

**red food coloring**

**3½ oz canned water chestnuts, drained and diced**

**3 tablespoons tapioca flour**

**3 cups water,**

*For the syrup*

**½ cup water**

**scant ½ cup white sugar**

*To serve*

**½ cup coconut cream**

**crushed ice**

*Serves 4*

Add a few drops of red food coloring to a bowl of water, then add the water chestnuts, and stir until the color soaks into them. Drain well.

Put the tapioca flour in a large plastic bag. Add the water chestnuts and shake the bag until they are evenly coated. Tip the water chestnuts into a strainer and shake until the excess tapioca flour falls off.

Bring the water to a boil in a pan over high heat. Add the water chestnuts and continue boiling for 2–3 minutes until the coating becomes clear. Drain the chestnuts, then put them under cold running water until they separate, and drain again. Shake dry and set aside.

To make the syrup, stir the sugar into the water in a small pan over high heat. Stir until the sugar dissolves, then leave to bubble until a syrup forms. Remove the pan from the heat and leave the syrup to cool.

Once the syrup is cool, stir in the water chestnuts. Transfer to individual bowls and top each with about 1 tablespoon coconut cream (according to taste) and crushed ice.

This is the best-known traditional Thai dessert there is. During my childhood, I always ate it for tea, which was straight after school—only a few hours before dinner. It is my most favorite dessert of all. Don't forget to allow plenty of time to soak the rice before steaming.

# Fresh Thai Mango with Sweet Sticky Rice

Khao-Neow Ma-Moung

½ quantity Steamed Sticky Rice (page 106)

½ teaspoon white sugar

a pinch of salt

2 fresh sweet mangoes

*For the marinade*

½ cup canned coconut milk, unshaken

1 pandanus leaf, cleaned, wiped dry, and tied into a knot (optional)

¼ cup white sugar

a pinch of salt

*For the decoration*

1 teaspoon dry-roasted sesame seeds or mung beans (without the green peel)

Sweet Golden Threads (page 138; optional)

*Serves 4*

To make the marinade, reserve 2 tablespoons of the coconut cream from the top of the can and heat the rest of the milk in a pan over medium heat. When the coconut milk is hot, stir in the pandanus leaf and simmer for about 3 minutes until it releases its aroma. Remove and discard the leaf, then stir in the sugar and salt, stirring until the sugar dissolves.

Place the steamed sticky rice in a large bowl and pour in the coconut-milk marinade. Stir well to mix together. Cover the bowl with plastic wrap and leave the rice to absorb all the marinade, which should take no longer than 20 minutes. Remove the plastic wrap and set the dessert aside to cool.

To make the thick coconut cream topping, put the 2 tablespoons of reserved coconut cream in a small bowl and warm quickly in a microwave. Add the sugar and salt, stirring until the sugar dissolves. Set aside to cool.

To prepare the mangoes, cut each mango from the thick side, slicing close to the pit, then repeat on the other side. Remove the skin and slice each side into 4 or 5 slices.

To serve, arrange the mango slices on a plate, then add the sweet sticky rice, and top with the sweetened coconut cream. Sprinkle with sesame seeds or mung beans and Sweet Golden Threads, if using.

The width of the pot you use to make the thick syrup will determine the length of the threads, so choose a wide pot to give you plenty of long threads. You can make the threads up to a few days in advance and store them in the refrigerator until you are ready to use them.

Enjoy this dish on its own as a proper dessert, or use it as a topping for coconut or vanilla ice cream. It also goes very well with Baked Egg Custard with Palm Sugar and Coconut Cream (opposite).

# Sweet Golden Threads

Foi-Thong

2½ cups white sugar

2 cups water

a few drops jasmine fragrance concentrate (optional)

10 egg yolks

Serves 6–8

First, make the thick syrup for the egg yolks to be cooked in. Mix the sugar and water in the widest pan or wok you have over high heat, stirring until the sugar dissolves. Stir in the jasmine fragrance concentrate, if using. Bring the syrup to a boil without stirring, then reduce the heat, and simmer for 25–30 minutes until it is quite thick. Keep the temperature stable so the syrup just lightly bubbles.

While the syrup is simmering, put the egg yolks in a bowl and gently stir them together so there aren't any bubbles. This is an important step. Line a strainer with a large piece of cheesecloth, pour the egg yolks into the cloth, and then wrap the cloth around the yolks. Gently squeeze the egg yolks through the cloth into a bowl. This makes sure the texture is as smooth as possible.

Put a small amount of the egg yolks in a cone-shaped funnel that is small enough for you to hold in one hand with your finger blocking the small hole in the tip while you spoon in the egg yolks. Once you have enough egg yolks in the cone to fill it, hold the cone high above the pan of bubbling syrup (the higher, the thinner the threads will be), unblock the cone, and, with a quick motion, keep the cone moving backward and forward from one end of the pan to the other until all the egg yolk has been used.

Once the egg yolks form into the string shape (it takes only a few seconds), lower the heat, and use chopsticks to pick up the egg threads quickly. Position another chop stick over an empty container and hang the egg-yolk threads over the chopstick to let the excess syrup drip off. Then drain the threads on paper towels.

Continue making egg-yolk threads until all the egg yolks are used. Each time you fill up the cone with more egg yolk, turn up the heat under the syrup before you release the yolk, otherwise the threads will turn out lumpy. Then reduce the heat each time you remove the cooked threads.

This dessert is normally sprinkled with fried shallots, but I prefer it without. The leftover coconut milk can be stored for later use.

This is a lovely dessert to enjoy in the winter. It can also be made with sweet potatoes instead of pumpkin.

# Baked Egg Custard with Palm Sugar and Coconut Cream

Kha-Noum Moor-Khang Kai

# Pumpkin in Warm Coconut Milk

Fak-Thong Kaeng-Buat

**scant 2 cups coconut cream from 3–4 x 14 fl oz unshaken cans of coconut milk**

**scant ¾ cup palm sugar**

**1 tablespoon all-purpose flour**

**7 eggs**

**Sweet Golden Threads (page 138; optional)**

*Serves 4*

Preheat the oven to 350°F. Put the coconut cream, palm sugar, and flour in a bowl and use your hands to mix together. In a separate bowl, beat the eggs until they are well blended and smooth.

Stir both mixtures together in a pan over medium heat, stirring constantly for about 10 minutes until the palm sugar is totally dissolved. Be careful not to heat the mixture for too long or the eggs will start to cook.

Pour the mixture into a 5 x 5 x 1¾-inch ovenproof dish and bake it for 40–45 minutes until the top becomes golden brown and the mixture sets.

Sprinkle the Sweet Golden Threads over the dish, if you like, and let cool before serving.

**2½ cups coconut milk**

**½ cup sugar**

**a pinch of salt**

**18 oz pumpkin, peeled and cut into pieces about ¾ x ½ inch**

*Serves 4*

Bring the coconut milk, sugar, and salt to a boil in a large pan over medium heat. Add the pumpkin pieces and continue simmering for about 8 minutes until they are tender, but still holding their shape.

Transfer to individual bowls and serve.

This dessert should taste sweet and slightly salty. It is delicious if you add corn kernels, but if you use canned kernels make sure they are well drained. In Thailand we use small green bananas called *gluay nam wa*, which have a firmer, finer texture than the long, yellow bananas found in western countries, although the recipe is the same!

Palm sugar has a smooth, coconut taste, unlike the sharp sweetness of white sugar. It is usually used in Thai desserts, as well as some savory dishes, especially curries. Look for palm sugar in Thai supermarkets—if you don't have any, use ordinary light brown sugar, but use less, as it is sweeter and sharper in taste.

## Bananas in Warm Coconut Milk

Gluay Buat-Chee

2½ cups coconut milk

1 pandanus leaf, cleaned, wiped dry, and tied into a knot (optional)

½ cup white sugar

¼ teaspoon salt

3 firm bananas, peeled, cut in half lengthwise, and each cut into 6–8 pieces

*Serves 4–6*

Bring the coconut milk to a boil in a pan over medium heat. Add the pandanus leaf, if using, then stir in the sugar and salt. Add the banana pieces and simmer for about 2 minutes until the bananas are tender. Discard the pandanus leaf and serve immediately.

## Chilled Melon in Coconut Milk and Palm Sugar

Tang Tai Naam Ga-Ti

1 cup coconut milk

1 cup water

4 tablespoons palm sugar or 3 tablespoons light brown sugar

a pinch of salt

5½ oz peeled melon, such as Cantaloupe, seeded and diced

crushed ice, to serve

*Serves 4*

Bring the coconut milk and water to a boil in a pan over medium heat. Stir in the palm or brown sugar and the salt, then remove the pan from the heat and let cool. Once the mixture is completely cool, you can chill it in the refrigerator for later use, if you choose.

To serve, put the melon in a large bowl and pour the coconut milk mixture over it. Sprinkle a little crushed ice over the top and serve.

# Index